God Is.

God Is.

My Search for Faith in a Secular World

DAVID ADAMS
RICHARDS

DOUBLEDAY CANADA

Doubleday Canada and colophon are trademarks

Library and Archives of Canada Cataloguing in Publication has
been applied for

ISBN: 978-0-385-66651-0

Printed and bound in the USA

Published in Canada by Doubleday Canada,
a division of Random House of Canada Limited

Visit Random House of Canada Limited's website: www.randomhouse.ca

10 9 8 7 6 5 4 3 2 1

For my sisters,
Susan Marshall
and Mary Jane Richards,

and for my sons,
John and Anton,

in love.

Introduction.

This is not a book that sets out to prove the existence of God, nor does it ask anyone to believe in any certain dogma. It is not a book about one faith, or one church—though I mention more than others my own church, which I fell away from and have struggled to come back to—an ongoing struggle, I assure you.

It is a book that simply states God is present, and always was and will be whether we say we have faith or not, whether we observe His presence or scorn His presence. It is a book that says faith is an inherently essential part of our existence, and it cannot be eradicated from our being. That even those who decry it and mock it, in some ways, embrace it totally, and every day millions of millions of men and women are, if only for a flickering moment, ennobled and set free because of it. And no one, no matter how great, whosoever denied it, ever really overcame it.

Part 1

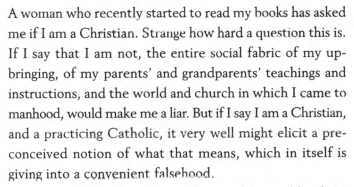

A woman who recently started to read my books has asked me if I am a Christian. Strange how hard a question this is. If I say that I am not, the entire social fabric of my up-bringing, of my parents' and grandparents' teachings and instructions, and the world and church in which I came to manhood, would make me a liar. But if I say I am a Christian, and a practicing Catholic, it very well might elicit a pre-conceived notion of what that means, which in itself is giving into a convenient falsehood.

So I could say that I am a Christian but not like those other Christians, or that I am a Catholic but not like some of those other Catholics. So already, I have hedged my bets and placed a stiff tariff on my own answer in order to be polite. It would be judging others, as I was afraid this very nice young woman would judge me. It would be judging in order not to be judged, to not willingly disclose who I am. Something like Saint Peter. (That, I suppose, is where our similarities end.)

But then I should not be so frightened of her question. And I should try to answer it this way:

"Do I believe in God? Far more now than when I was 20, far more than when I was 35, and I hope not as much as when I am 70."

"And have you done serious wrong?"

"I have done serious wrong many times—but God, I'm afraid, had nothing to do with it."

In our own time, in the century just ended, no one denied God's existence more than Joseph Stalin. To my mind, the Soviet dictator is far more than anyone else the key, the lesson, for people to ponder when they doubt the existence of God.

State-enforced atheism existed in the Soviet Union for years. In fact, God was the last thing Stalin ever needed, until God was the last thing he had.

After Hitler launched Operation Barbarossa on June 22, 1941, Stalin opened the churches, knowing his army fought not only on their stomach. The political survivor knew the only way to save Russia was through the faith of its people. That no matter the square blocks of bleak buildings that came to be known after his own name, he could not erase their faith in a Being greater than himself. So cynicism won the day.

But to be fair to Stalin, it was only a stop-gap, a little glitch in his overall testimony against Christ himself. He had many more battles to wage against Christ. Still, in 1941 it was a wise decision. And completely self-interested. That is what is so brilliant about it. Church became his own vehicle to ride out the madness, while planes of the Luftwaffe bombed and strafed his people.

The churches were opened to save Mother Russia. Who wouldn't do that? But then again, what choice did he himself have?

Stalin did quite well at coming to terms with his own peculiar brand of nihilism early in life—cynicism propelled him past every one of his comrades—yet what is important here is that he could never elude the presence of Something else.

This Something plagued him from the time he was a boy. This was to become his greatest personal struggle. In a way, he took the entire Soviet Union into his confidence about his need to create nothing out of something. And it is fascinating to witness, for in so many respects it defines who we are as well. It tells us enough about our own dialogue with Something to make us thank Stalin, in a way, for showing us what not to question. For this Something was a painful presence to him, and it led him into areas of the human conscience where no man should dare go.

If we rely upon myth for just a second, he truly was like one of the great angels who in torment questioned the power and the grace of what could flick him like a gnat, yet he continued to believe in his own indispensability. In moments he almost confided in it like an older brother. The country was bled to death because of it. And still this Something persisted.

Stalin fought these doubts about the nothing of nothing all of his life. The entire Soviet Union was a testimony to his great battle against this Something.

Without the blink of an eye, Uncle Joe signed orders to have men he had dined with executed because nothing meant nothing. But still, what was behind it all? And more to the point, why do we need Nothing? Why do we seek it? What good will it do us?

How much better off will we be if we find it?

Nothing begets nothing. "Our nada who art in nada," as Ernest Hemingway reminds us.

Hemingway, of course, believed in humanity. But humanity, as a stable of man's divinity, still rankled Stalin. Stalin became ruthlessly proficient at deploring humanity, and tried his best to excise it from the common bones of the proletariat. His professed love of them was godlike except for one thing—forgiveness. Every man, woman, and child was under his thumb, and it was a big thumb. And every deficiency had something to do with the soul.

People who decry the crimes of Stalin tout the idea and even deity of his arch-enemy Trotsky, who Stalin managed to kill, the assassin arriving in Mexico with a Canadian passport. But if Stalin was the brutal arm of revolution, Trotsky was its cerebral death mask. Both by 1921 were mass murderers.

What both needed to rid Russia of was never called humanity. It was called treason, or counter-revolution, the kulaks, bourgeois, or priestly hypocrisy. It had dozens of names. By the end of the reign of Beria, Stalin's number-one executioner, maybe thousands. But looking deep into the soul, what Stalin hated all had to do with gentleness and humanity. It was even a snit at the possibility that people were stupid enough to believe him. As if to say, How dare the peasants be so gullible as to think this revolution had anything to do with them? That, in fact, was why his second wife, the one he loved, Nadia, shot herself. She was the real proletariat of the household.

A friend once said to me that the Eastern theatre was where the real war took place and the Battle of Britain was a sideshow. Yet, in some way, I have come to realize it was all a sideshow. Something much greater was going on. And that the battles we engage in as humans are a constant sideshow.

There is always something else far more important at stake. The human soul, in some ways like good helium, expands to whatever environment it has. Or conversely sinks into whatever ditch it is offered. That's where the real battles are waged—and waged continually.

Stalin's war was fought against the very presence of God. Goebbels might have said that Hitler was too great a man to be compared to Christ, but we think of Stalin as the man who needed to obliterate him.

It was a lonely war—against God. That is what makes Stalin fascinating to us. Like Satan in *Paradise Lost*, beating his wings as he flies through the great caverns toward the hopeful decimation of earth, a heroic figure. Yet at the last, faced with another pagan of equal force—an enemy at the gates so monstrous it was as if they were twins—he called on God to help his soldiers fight, granting them to call on *Him*. The great patriotic war was really the great holy war. And after allowing prayer and Communion, he then tossed God away again.

To eradicate God was not to make men equal—this is what many of us always pretend or are deluded by. The wisdom of those who have come to the conclusion that there is nothing but themselves have in the end usually little generosity to spare the masses. Even in the tavern talk of certain friends of the seventies, the new world, where we were all equal, where women were as capable as men of denouncing humanity (which was considered grave intelligence), there was always the idea that some would have to be eradicated, or left on the sidelines, or at least see our point of view. The secret we failed to grasp was that the only way we seemed able to have someone equal to ourselves was to diminish anyone who disagreed with us.

The great misconception of Stalin or anyone else is that equality finally rids one of the need for faith.

The French Revolution's Reign of Terror in all its frantic bloodletting shows us that man never considered men (or women) equal, just as the war against God in the 1930s and 1940s in Russia was done in the end to make Stalin God.

I wrote in one of my novels that Stalin, Koba the Dread, would never have stopped until there was no one left on the face of the earth but himself. He could never have been happy until this happened. Happy, of course, is relative. This internecine gorge and flicking off of the human substance was hellish in its design. The idea of human character was to be smashed to atoms, and the revolution was to end with Stalin as sole proprietor of the world. He threw his entire country into chambers in hell and watched as they writhed, like men on racks, trying to behold him. Letters from those dying men and women poured forth, begging for mercy, for exile, and for one more glimpse of his face.

They had made a choice and it was deliberate. At the last moment they knew they had killed easily and humorously for the man about to kill them easily and humorously. Suddenly they knew how intricately hell worked. But even if he had managed to eradicate all those other humans he would have been left entirely on his own, with that something he still spoke to. That something he refused to call God. Because that's what it was all about.

Stalin's final moments have been revealed to us by his daughter Svetlana and by his doctors and confidants. Suddenly at the end (or, just perhaps, the beginning), a look of terror and rage crossed over his face. He was looking up toward the far ceiling, and he lifted himself up and shook his fist at Something. It seemed that his seventy-four years of life on this "scrap of earth," as Tolstoy called it, had not really prepared him for what was about to come.

However, as always, none of us knows.

Beria confidently prepared the state funeral, assuming the reign of terror would continue under his direction. But he was arrested, tied and gagged, put up on a hook, and, while trying to scream, shot in the forehead without the least mercy.

On Khrushchev's orders.

After his wife congratulated him on becoming Supreme Soviet, Khrushchev simply said, "I am up to my armpits in blood."

That is, he knew how it had all worked.

––––

I mention this at the start of this little book because, to me, nothing proves the existence of God more. And in a way it provides a few answers. One, how easy man slides when he wishes to deny God. And two, how close Stalin and Beria are to us. They are archetypal figures for our recent global history—they were supreme. And evil, if evil can ever be fully described. Yet when you read their cant and posture, their sniggering, they are our neighbours and ourselves at our lowest moments.

When I read about these leaders and their subordinates— the pettiness toward those out of favour, the forced morality of those who hold reign, the obsequiousness of those wanting favour—they come very close to us. Even Stalin's brutality is only that of a man frightened of losing.

Where do you say, Could we ever see this in ourselves? One only has to look at the movie *Glengarry Glen Ross*. It is a movie made in 1992 that deals with the cutthroat world of real estate in Arizona. The great line, when Jack Lemmon is refused a cup of coffee, "Coffee's for closers only, " is a line that could be used by any one of Stalin's subordinates. Al Pacino's character trying to con his mark into counting four days as only three, and almost succeeding, is much like the notion of lying to change the order of the universe. And Jack Lemmon, at the end, begging Kevin Spacey to take twenty-five hundred dollars that he has stolen as a bribe shows that they had become, in spite of themselves, a nest of vipers. And yet we still in some way have compassion for them because we see them in ourselves.

That is most of this behaviour can be seen on a daily basis—vying for attention and resenting and manipulating.

For it wasn't the great things that brought them to where they were, but the small day-to-day mendacities. Stalin forcing Khrushchev to step-dance at the dacha at two in the morning is somehow, in a strange way, proof of the demonic. And reverses Talleyrand's assertion about Napoleon's terrible mistake in killing a political rival: That it wasn't a crime but a blunder to the mirror opposite; it wasn't a blunder but a crime.

Banal? Absolutely. Trite? Of course. Apocalyptic? Certainly.

The banality of evil, Hannah Arendt suggested when looking upon Adolf Eichmann.

"She was talking not about us as being evil, but only the supreme characters," an acquaintance of mine said.

People do believe that evil is always about the big deeds. And sainthood is almost always pious and absurd, with the accent on "absurd," and most often caricatured or lampooned, with the accent on "lampooned." As a general rule, this trivializing of religious edicts on good and bad is considered just because of some unknown personal injury that we manufacture continually within the hubris of moral relativism.

There are reasons for this, which the church is in some way responsible, for it browbeat us too much. It is of course what Stalin himself would consider as true. If anything, he was party to the big deeds—absolutely. Yet we might reflect that he punished all the little ones—even killed the parents of a girl who dared have her picture taken with him.

For the most part, we accept our opinion about ourselves, and not only believe it, but on a daily basis seem to prove it out. And by this, I mean, that it might be Stalin who is evil, not us.

To think about evil on a day-to-day basis is to question our own motives in certain things where we too would act like those seeking favour with demigods. Still and all, this is why I chose Stalin to start this book.

Nor am I at all asking us to look upon ourselves as evil! I am asking, however, to entertain the idea that evil does exist, and is not exclusive to the German or Russian, or the English or Dutch. Or the American or Pakistani, either.

For if we do not want to compare ourselves to those hopeless people, Stalin's forlorn subordinates, then it is best we do not consider our flaws as being such as would consolidate us to them in any way whatsoever.

"Oh it is the same, but only to a degree," my friends might say.

But I say, as Mortimer Adler does, that the degree does not negate the similarity—only a difference in kind can do this—and our actions, compared to millions before us, are not at all a difference in kind, but only a difference to a degree. And this is fatal when we try to dismiss it as being unimportant in a matter of faith or God.

But why did I decide to write this book in the first place? It will only get me in trouble with friends who think I am already far too conservative for my own good. And why would one want to think about it? Not thinking about it gets us along just fine. In fact much of what people on the left believe I believe as well. And much of what they desire I desire also. But I feel they cannot achieve these things without faith. And I believe most of them upon reflection realize this. Nor am I saying the left does not have faith—that would be profoundly stupid. But I will say there is a secular trend today to keep faith as far away from us as possible.

Most of the people I know do not consider a study of faith or believing in God to be very important. We have put those notions to rest, or at least recognize that they are safely beyond us now. And in many ways I do not blame them—for it is a quagmire.

Still most of us, myself included, have a little faith left. It clings to our deepest hopes, just a tad. But that is okay. For any degree of faith, any at all, tells us in so many ways that it is false not to think of faith as relevant. Faith tells us that the quagmire we are in has nothing to do with faith. Even bad religions have nothing to do with faith.

Then what does faith provide that helps us to make a start on achieving what we say we want to achieve? Anything? Well, maybe just one thing.

Faith allows us peace only from the active, complicit role of wrongful injury. That does not allow us much, it seems. Very little. But still, that is just about the only thing it promises. And I might add this: that guarantee is a good thing, even if we have to work at it on a daily basis. And even if we see many who give up faith and become complicit in wrongful injury. So my contention is that those of us who want to maim or kill in the name of faith have in fact given it up, and put their faith, even for a limited time, in their own hubris or in mimicking the hubris of others they admire.

That is, if we start by actually admitting that faith can help us overcome ourselves enough not to injure others—then faith can provide everything else, by and by. We couldn't slaughter a million men, could we? Well, Strelnikov, the poor character in *Doctor Zhivago*, thought he could not either, until he realized that he had to give up notions of fairness (and faith—even faith—in what he once believed he was doing) or be crucified.

In fact, this is the place where I might say the Gospel hints at the same thing—that is, the choice given to us at birth. Hardly any of us have opted for the second option. And there are many ways to be crucified. All of us have faced some of these ways, and if you are like me, most of us have balked.

So we make up reasons why we don't need to have faith. We have continuous self-explanations as to why our faith no longer matters. But if faith does not matter, no matter if we are conservative or liberal, our ideas and ideals (which in many respects are the same) cannot be achieved. If they could be achieved without faith, they would have been by now. We continually make the same mistakes, hoping for different results.

But if by chance faith does matter, then we might see it in startling ways. A man with his children in a small wagon moving through a battlefield seems more important to the vastness of space and time than the dragoons fighting the rearguard action.

Still, I suppose it is very hard to convince those who are fighting.

I believe that the main thing any of us has fought over throughout our history is God or the lack of God, or the reasons why God agrees with us instead of them. But, as the man with the children in his wagon might show, that is not at all God's fault.

———

I decided to write this book because over the last number of years I realized I did not agree with the faithful (or at least all they said), so much as disagree with the unfaithful (or those who say they do not have faith). That is, sooner or later one has to answer those who make it a point of saying that you and most of those you love are wrong. What I believe cannot of course be proven, but there are some things that my life allows me to believe, and nothing anyone has ever said has done anything to change this. For instance, there is a scene from my life that I have held on to, even in my despair. My mother, years and years ago, was at the cottage alone with the children. She had made a fire and roasted marshmallows with us, on a Tuesday night. Then she put what she thought were the cold coals outside, behind the house. At eleven o'clock she went to bed. At eleven o'clock my father, in another town, woke, and suddenly decided to get dressed and drive to see us. That is something he almost never did that late. This is a very simple story— a complete coincidence, I know—like the ones we hear about, of knockings and portents. Yet his decision saved the life of his family. And it is that simple. We were allowed by Something beyond ourselves to live. And if we had not been, then it was willed or allowed that we were not. Why? Because we had absolutely no choice ourselves. Coincidences, as G.K. Chesterton tells us, are spiritual puns.

Faith, I know, is pretty simple, and that is why it is considered at times simple-minded. But it is not. Nothing anyone has yet argued has convinced me that what intellectuals consider simple-minded is not the clarity required for the sublime.

Some years ago a CBC commentator suggested to a Nobel Prize laureate that we ourselves had become God, or god-like, because everything was now possible, and we could reasonably assume we were superior to the silly superstition and blind ego that caused the church to maintain that the sun revolved about the earth. (This idea that the church had not progressed implies that God Himself had not passed basic geometry and did not know what Galileo did. It also implies rather smugly that our ideas are now much superior to the humanity that created Michelangelo and Leonardo, or for that matter, Galileo himself.)

The commentator believed he had said it to a receptive guest, a physicist.

Yet the commentator was surprised to discover that the physicist actually disagreed with him. With a good deal of humility not shared by his host, he said that he never felt that this was the case, that he believed in the existence of God, and that, for him, science actually proved it.

How? Well, for one thing, not a molecule in the universe seemed to him out of place, as random as that place appeared. That the astral belt prevented us from being decimated, as much as our peculiar distance from the sun. That the degree to which the world turned on its axis provided us with life, no scientist could ever imagine or impart without a greater design. That, in fact, if there was a degree of change in anything, the whole place would fall flat on its face. And since the commentator at the CBC had not himself ordered this, and, what is more, would never understand it, then just perhaps he might not consider himself God. "We are we, and God is God," the gentleman said.

Hilarious? Probably. Refutable?

Well, you can refute a televangelist who believes his grandfather walked with the brachiosaurus, but a physicist who has given his life to the prospect that the universe might have soluble equations that has an intelligence as great as the cosmos we wallow in is a different kettle.

But there is another more subtle and less admitted strand here, because it is less admirable. The commentator was in certain respects giving into the standards, as changeable as they were, of the Soviet dictator himself—that we have the power to become God. (Stalin believed, a month before his death, exactly what his doctors told him: he would live at least 150 years.)

And this coincides with the views of some of our modern novelists and thinkers. That is, that our intellect invented God and not the other way around.

It is an egalitarian idea to believe that no one who wishes equality would ever admit God exists. God, throughout the centuries, persecutes. Well it is my belief that though life can be terrible it is not because God ever persecutes us. He persecutes no-one. And in fact there is as much persecution among our egalitarians as among anyone else.

But I am in a strange position as a writer.

God never fares at all well in work beyond the latter part of the nineteenth century, except perhaps for Solzhenitsyn whose work is looked upon with great skepticism now. Or in books that actually define and delineate the greater agony of the human spirit, like Malcolm Lowry's *Under the Volcano*— as great and as funny as most books written, even those books that are considered funny first.

Lowry at one point writes that man's tragedy is in that place once known as the soul. Here, Lowry is not giving the soul up, not at all, he is lamenting that the world has. But this is as far as most writers, even those I much admire like Lowry, are willing to take it. My point here is not to say one has to promote religion in order to create, my point is that so many artists now believe that the mention of God harms their creation, and that the dismissal or disrespect of that which is associated with God enlivens it. In the last three years I have read five novels by students of mine in which mocking irreverence is shown toward religious people (most often but not always Catholic). They think this is somehow revolutionary and inspired—rather than old hat and insipid.

In point of fact, it would be far more acceptable for some to hear they were like Joe Stalin, than for anyone to say that they were like an Anglican minister or, God forbid, a Catholic priest.

Still, why do some think (or, in fact, demand) there is no God? One reason is that because the universe is so incomprehensible to us, we cannot imagine how it could be organized with Intellect. So therefore to some of us, it is not organized with Intellect, and we use our intellect, which we fully admit is limited, to verify this lack of causality. But where did our own intellect come from? Nothing—which is the atheist's belief. Yet he is the first to ascribe to the tenet that there is no intelligent design to the universe because, of course, nothing can come out of nothing.

———

As I stated, I came in my own halting way back to faith not because of those who believed, but because of those who did not. I believed faith did not keep us from sin—or if we want to call it by another name, wrongdoing—but it helped us combat it, and that without it, if it was truly absent, the world of our psyche would spiral into chaos. That faith is a necessary component within our very fabric. Faith will never answer the question of why. But faith in some way proves it. Why do we breathe and move and exist? Because of faith. Without it, nothing at all would ever happen. Not even this line I am writing now. Faith is the component that allows all the various organs to work. This, for me, is absolutely true. I came to believe it over time.

Back in 1969, the world of the university I went to writhed in popular dissention against everything. Most certainly religion. And so, by proxy, faith itself.

But it was not what the youth were against, for I was against much of it myself, but the alternative they offered that struck me as conventional and, in many respects, stupid. When the historian John Lukacs says that Trotsky was a fool, you can believe him. When I say that half the professors I met my first few years at university were stupid, please believe me. I have never in my life witnessed so much conformity among those who postured freedom, and measured a person's worth only on how much he or she was willing to conform. The very thing to which they were supposedly seeking an alternative.

Their alternative was one where authority was no longer relevant. In order to prove ourselves, we must agree with those who insisted on its irrelevance. That is, we had to affirm our consensus or be dismissed authoritatively by those who wanted to quash all authority. And certain professors were in positions of authority to tell us this. (Nor is the situation completely dissimilar today.)

This was the staple of many who went to university, who suddenly assumed a pejorative position about the home and the parents they had been nurtured by. But they still insisted upon the authority they themselves set against those they deemed untrustworthy. This was in the end a fanatical double-dealing for power that helped define and, in many respects, destroy the integrity of many of my generation.

This anomaly has stuck with me for my entire life—this diet of hard dissent against so much that did many of them no harm, cost so many of them so little, except for a loss of personal integrity. And it was the personal integrity of many, which I questioned, which over a long agonizing time brought me back, veering this way and that, careening ever so clumsily, to the idea that God lives and breathes in us all, and not to realize this is to coat ourselves with a veneer that hides the truth from others as well as ourselves. That the loss of our personal integrity is the signpost that allows for the slow decimation of the human spirit.

This was the dilemma my entire generation was placed in when I was eighteen. The idea that learning which was now being offered in the first great democratic fashion could easily quash the superstition of the past, lessen conflict, and resolve all issues. Man and woman would be equal and free. And supposedly one of the major reasons for this, hidden and yet open, was the seeking of sex and power. It sounds silly and simple but it was, simply put, that silly and simple. The most powerful thing, as Pascal said, in a democratic world is public opinion.

Public opinion stated that this was right, and worthy, and those who did not agree were unworthy. But to borrow from John Lukacs again, there was something more powerful than public opinion, and that was popular sentiment. The popular sentiment is slower to react, but many people understood these supposed liberal attitudes were in some ways bogus.

But for a long time public opinion was what it was. Freedom was sought by my generation, just as for every other generation. Still, there was one problem, a variation on the theme. My generation, in order to exhibit this freedom, spoke and acted in compliance to how they felt they should speak and act, more than any other generation, because they had succumbed to the power of others. In fact, you could say it became their religion to dress and act in the exact way their peers did, so as not to be, well, individual. To not be singled out, and crucified. It was a way to remove themselves from the pain of having to be themselves.

So if I disliked the disingenuousness of some religious people, I disliked the disingenuousness of these fellows more. Of course, the desire for sex and power was hidden within the supposedly moral search for a revolution to believe in, while faith instructed us to go in another direction. To become internal, not external. That is what faith asked.

So the combatants against authority combatted one of the things authority seemed to control within conventional day-to-day life—religion. The real and true instruction religion gave was deemed unnecessary. But the problem was it was deemed unnecessary even for many who believed in it, for they were told to believe in it was wrong.

Much of it was silly. But it was unfortunate how it was contrived as wisdom. How:

"If they could only kill the cops, the world would be safe," as one sociology professor said to us one night, as we sat about, sipping beers and brooding about the world. I looked at his thin shoulders, his sunken chest, and his groomed moustache. He, if that happened, wouldn't have lasted a moment with some of the people I knew. Survival of the fittest would really have been put to the test. What was worse is that the students sitting near me, almost all to a man or woman, advocated what he said out of a terrible convention and need to belong, and at the same time evoked a common dissent against people that I had grown up trusting—the rednecks.

It was thought to be a new gospel.

This easy yet hard-edged self-righteousness against those "others" who were self-righteous.

By that time I had known a few people who had committed murder and had seen men kicked to unconsciousness. I don't think many of those at the table had ever witnessed such things. Nor is this false bravado. I simply knew what they were saying about cops, or anyone else, was bogus. Years later, reading V. S. Naipaul's *A Bend in the River*, I realized the book evoked my feeling exactly in the scene where intellectuals are listening to modern songs and speaking in mild-mannered tones about violence and crisis while knowing they are safe themselves. It also revealed the duplicity of needing comfort for our pretence to understanding deprivation.

I left the table of my peers and walked home alone.

It was the beginning of my change, maybe an elemental

one. But one that is ongoing. No one saw this change inwardly, but outwardly they must have. For I became very unhappy with myself and those around me, and remained so for many years. I think it was from that time forward where I could no longer stand jokes about religion because they so often were cheap, and more than anything often cheapened the person telling them.

As Einstein said: "Christianity will never be explained away by a smart remark."

I became in some circles a social outcast and have remained so, not because I was so much wiser, or more in love with religion, but because I knew so much atheistic and social activism wasn't based on truth as much as compliance to the rather strict rules of social etiquette, which were both safe and popular—the very thing people deplored in others with authority. One only has to look back at the revolution of the sixties to know this.

Though I believed in the blood of the saints as true and sacred, nothing about religion pleased me either. And I had no avenue to worship. I did not go to church. Much of it, I felt, was hobbled by pettiness. And, to put it bluntly, I was lazy.

Only as time went on did I see that the world of faith was open-ended. How ever much one put into it, one received. This is what I had to acknowledge in order to forgo my reservations about it. When I did, the idea of religious people, of those who actually were (not those who used it for their own benefit), struck me as being grander and wiser, and they were actually more at peace than I had ever dreamed possible.

With faith, there must be a reason for things, as random as those things seemed.

I would think often in those days about a murder on my river that happened when I was a boy. It was, some said, a "wrong place at the wrong time" event. A man had gone into a garage to get something and was murdered, either in a case of mistaken identity or a random slaying by a shot in the dark through a window. So it seemed meaningless that his life was over.

Yet I kept coming back to the idea again and again, that this kind of event in a person's life cannot be random—and that a greater intelligence than our own must know this is not random, even if we take it as such—and from the moment our lives begin, hundreds of thousands of moments happen to us yearly the actual portent of which we do not understand.

I remember this plaguing me when I was nineteen. But it did not plague me because I could not see a great wisdom in it, but because in fleeting moments I could, and as a general rule what I thought to be the most serious observation was not taken seriously by people whose intelligence I trusted. Yet it was taken seriously by some who those intelligent friends would think they were superior to. Which I suppose should have been my first lesson in humility.

There were other things as well.

One of the things I defended was novel among my wise and brilliant friends. (And many of them were wise and brilliant.) I didn't want to start out having to defend this, but then again, I had to. You see, I had no choice, and still do not.

It was this: my girlfriend Peggy, who is now my wife, still went to Mass. This was not a big thing. Most people did not care. But the world is not made up of most people, and we were friends with certain people who (though I am sure they did not really care) saw this as a potential weakness to goad in us.

The idea was that she was being duped, and if she could learn from a certain number of our more progressive friends, she would soon know better. If they could get her away from me, the violent chauvinist that I was, she would be much better off.

That she never learned any better was always a bane even to our more tolerant friends, who as time went on we saw as intolerant of her. I had to defend her Catholicism because she was a target, and did not deserve to be belittled by them—something that the progressive-minded never quite seem to understand.

Even now, and with a kind of sorrowful distaste, I remember people who we considered true friends making utterly false statements about her Catholic religion in her presence as if they had carte blanche to do so.

But in a way they were not intolerant of her so much as me. I was the one they were after. That is, if I was interested in equality of women as they were, I would of course countermand her position and convince her she was in error for her own good. Which of course is what people in authority do. But, you see, it was something else, something both she and I noticed. They never spoke like this when they themselves were alone or outnumbered—always, the people I am speaking about were intellectually brave in a crowd—at a dinner party that we were invited to, and many like-minded people were at the table. Then they could pontificate, then they could be courageous.

This was the first major sticking point in my lesson of what tolerance was or should be when it concerned the confrontation of faith.

There is of course something else here. Many of my friends had switched jackets, but underneath their skin was exactly the same. They still needed to belong, and for the sake of personal prestige, they needed to scapegoat those who didn't belong. They were like high school jocks. That is unfair to the jocks. Still, they needed God. Just as every person I have ever met needs God. Most were just wanting to join the most fashionable God around—as Pierre Berton said, "the most comfortable pew." Growing up, I knew people from all walks of life, and all religions—Pentecostal to practising Catholic—and for the most part, most of them were every bit as wise as the sociology professor I mentioned. In fact, most of them were wiser.

I realized by 1970 that even if I didn't believe in God (and I was never sure even at my most unsure whether I did or did not when I was twenty) I would never again ridicule those who sought a God.

For a long, long time, it was a seemingly pointless and silly stand to defend those who went to church or had faith. Of course this did not always come up, and sometimes when it did, it was only in slight or irrelevant ways. And many times I did not bother to defend it at all. Still and all, there was an understanding, unspoken or not, that where the real people, and free people, and advanced people were concerned, faith was the pasty artifice of past generations, easily proven false, and any really progressive person would understand this entirely. But since it had never been proven false to me, I was not so easily convinced. So I would remind some of them that faith might not be at all worthless, and God might not be false. Some put up with me, and others knew it as well to be true. Many I suppose had much more faith than I did.

And as I said earlier, on many occasions this never came up in such a way as to create an argument. Still to have faith was to some to disagree with the new world, with their ideas of equality and feminism, their peace movement and social activism, which were all staples of a literary community I wanted to belong to. My faith, or really it wasn't my faith, only my questioning of those who dismissed it, was not only irrelevant or trifling. It became after a time, among some men and women (not all) I really cared for, seditious to the new ideologies that they believed literary theory had inherited by a gigantic struggle against an inhibiting and paternalistic religion. But to dismiss faith because you had once been taught by a sanctimonious priest, seemed as in error as anything a false doctrine might say. "Sanctimony" is the word we must examine, for it crosses the boundaries of and cuts a swath through both the religious and secular world—and most of us know it when we see it.

So over time it became my refusal to mock, because I had mocked before and knew the price paid not only by the poor man I mocked, but myself the mocker, that cast me as an outsider in a certain way. Still what was I refusing to mock?

It was in fact one thing only. A person's right to believe, which to me is sacrosanct to a person's humanity. A person's right to believe. That is all.

But more importantly, a person's right not to be ostracized because of it.

That is all it was. So that meant that a person should not object to the religion of a Jew, a Muslim, a Christian.

That's not much, but it allowed me to navigate at a distinct disadvantage for the longest time. For the mocking of belief is really a disapproval of one person's belief, and a public display and certitude of that disapproval by those who have sanctioned another kind of belief. And it is this certitude of disapproval which is often more than mildly sanctimonious. And it is the same sanctimony many of those who ostracize belief are themselves pretending to deride. That to me was not a little problem, but indeed a very grave one.

When I was seventeen, I happened to be in a car accident. I was travelling very fast one night and flipped the car, end for end, when I hit water, and travelled upside down a good distance. The only thing that saved me was the fact that I had not fastened my seat belt. The top of the car was crushed on the driver's side to the point where it bent the steering wheel in two. If I had been wearing my seat belt, I would have been crushed. As it was, I let go of the steering wheel when the car was upside down, and landed in the back seat without a scratch. About the same time, a good friend of mine was killed, travelling at thirty miles an hour. The front wheel of his car went off the side of the road, and the sudden jostling drove his neck against the partially opened window, and broke it. He was killed instantly.

I wondered often about the idea of equality—after this—and what equality actually meant. I have been surrounded by the death of the young in my life, and in every way so many of them had so much to offer. I have never come to terms with the fact that people believe there is a way to equality without faith. I did not start out thinking this, but the death of some around me made me realize nothing can be taken for granted, not even a moment, and so equality must come from somewhere else. Of course, we all know this. But it is a truism that should be revisited now and again. When young people sometimes do daring things and then brag that they have "cheated death," it might be better if they realized they were allowed to. In fact, the very idea of being a rogue and defying death might have far less rebellion in it than the rogue pretends. At some moment in his curious endeavour, he might realize that all that will happen is now out of his control, and he might offer a secret prayer to the great unknown Entity he is intent on defying.

The equality sought in university had many hard edges and exclusionary clauses. It was at times the egalitarian ideal of the dumbing down of the human spirit.

For instance, the sociology professor who was a mainstay to uninhibited behaviour would seek equality for a woman to be a scientist or have an abortion, but how dare one say she prayed to God or sought even a different attitude toward humanity in her study than He deemed correct? It would always be a problem for him that women would not think the way he assumed their new liberty instructed them to. So my wife, and many others, would be excluded or bullied. Those were the options. For the professor to talk about sexism or sects condescendingly and not to mention his attitude as both was a convenience born of his entitlement.

But there is something else that I think allows us to dismiss faith. Convention. And why do I say this? Because those who succumbed to popular afflictions, alcohol and drugs, often were very early set on the road to self-destruction by being told they were doing what had to be done to shake away convention, and ended up acting with the principles they were given, and they did so only to belong—so others would have faith in them. That is, there is a real problem of conformity among the rebellious. Tolstoy makes brave and wonderful statements in two of his shorter novels about this. In both Tolstoy's *The Death of Ivan Ilyich* and *The Kreutzer Sonata*, Tolstoy takes apart convention and the utter falseness of convention in the face of death, and asks us to re-examine what convention actually does to straitjacket our lives, to make us less free and less human by our need to be approved of by other people, and forgo faith. For the forgoing of faith is most often more the conformist's way than not.

It is and was no different then than now. Convention that created the "comfortable pew" also created the comfortable agnostic.

I have discovered that the world we live in is the same throughout the ages. Nor is it as Samuel Beckett says, "a brief light at the foot of a grave." It would be that and could be, except for one thing. And it is what I began to realize after a time, sitting with those who would disagree with me.

It is this:

Not one of us doesn't pray to God continually—even if it is only to tell God to go to hell, that we need our tenure and our research money. That is I believe that the conversations we hold by ourselves are always with God. (The idea that atheism is considered by law a religion in the United States might seem peculiar but it does show something about what I have been saying.)

So the one thing I re-learned at university I had learned in my adolescence when I was rolling a car at 110 miles an hour. And it was this—the only time man pretends he does not need God is when he thinks or she thinks they are themselves God or are in a position of such comfort that God cannot trouble them or touch them. Once the man or woman finds himself or herself in deep trouble or despair, they search for what was always there.

What was/is always there? This is the ancient Greek sophistry that has eloped throughout the centuries, always our bride or bridegroom. Suddenly Aladdin with his pints of gold has no use for Deity. Suddenly Aladdin cries for God once the magic carpet begins to tumble from the sky.

So here are those moments I come back to: an accident that I had utterly no control over, rolling a car end over end at 110 miles an hour, and for all intents and purposes I should be dead; and my good friend's tire hitting the soft shoulder at thirty miles an hour, and for all intents and purposes he should be alive. Neither of us seemed to have any choice in the matter. No. None at all. Now does this make me any better than that boy? Not at all. He was one of the finest and most gentle kids I knew, in ways far kinder than I have ever managed to be. And as Mark Twain said about kindness, it is "the language the deaf can hear and the blind can see." So my friend's life was at least equal to mine, and in many respects his death as significant as any other.

Within Canada's writing and intellectual community, many people I know will not examine the idea of skepticism toward the existence of God as not being absolutely progressive. It is a credulity of thought that is almost prerequisite in much of our literary culture. Darwin proved it, or someone proved it, and now our literary quest is to make such proof absolute. The derision toward anyone who believes, or toward any other proof, is swift and non-negotiable in many people writing today. Or at least in their writing. It is as if a doctrine has been set in motion where not to demean religion is sacrilegious. That is not to say I want anyone to write religious books. Far from it, let me tell you. Anyone who thinks that misses the point entirely. I am simply reflecting on the plethora of anti-religious elitism that passes for both comedy and concern among people who lecture from the stage. It is a kind of swaggering doctrine that in its own way is as rigid in its essential belief as the evangelical or Catholic dogma it mocks.

There is also a tendency on the left to believe that the very belief in God is itself too conservative or right wing to have intelligence, and to exhibit this belief by an unspoken condition of the left toward a comfortable agnostic pluralism.

Seeing the lunatic religious fringe, those who would burn our books and libraries, as a danger, there are some who have transposed this danger to anyone who disagrees with any value that the literary left deems safe. Of course the religious lunatic fringe would burn libraries and destroy freedoms that are established for the security of us all. But so would some of the literary left who believe only so-called politically correct writing to be fair writing—and this thinking can be extremely dangerous and limiting as well. In fact, I have noticed the same tendency in people who have the power to shape opinion about other people's work.

Their qualifying discretion is at times so dangerous and limiting that some who put juries together and judge awards believe that mentioning sin in a work is tantamount to—well, sin. It is this kind of thinking that is more noticeable among my peers than any other. And it is that way because books are, to some, supposed to be the answer to liturgy. Especially among some of my closer friends Catholic liturgy. In so many novels, the characters stand up against a predetermined set of values that the reader is familiar with, but has been taught by these books to fear, ridicule, and mistrust, even if, in private, many of the readers might in some ways trust and depend on the values castigated. So a falsehood is set in motion by the very presumption of casting out falsehood, and the reader is the vulnerable target. That certain writers I know and admire are prone to this duplicity is more upsetting than those fundamentalists I do not know, and do not admire telling me works of genius are false. For it so happens that people I admire who have found a comfortable niche in the writing community have said this as well, about certain works that I admire very much.

This anti-religious sniping has become more prevalent over my lifetime within the literary community because of a dual condition of pandering: one by the artists themselves to the audience; and the other by the audience's acceptance of this pandering as their due without seriously questioning any true benefit from it, so as not to displease others in the audience who they believe must share a common ideology. Only the middle class could act such to the middle class, and to deem that this pandering is somehow a forthright and noble condition for an ongoing discussion of justice. What is more distressing is that many will not admit to the discomfort they feel when they hear this creed spoken to them, for out of fear or disinterest, a stand against it is not within the boundary of their own moral compass.

So it becomes within the pandering elaborate an oxymoron to suggest that the ongoing search for justice has anything whatsoever to do with an ongoing search for God. They have become the antithesis of each other. This has been at least part of the mainstay of our literary jurisprudence since the fifties and is now so ingrained into the consciousness of young writers that many of them have found few independent ways to think of God, except to either dismiss or to rebuke. But even this in a strange way is an acknowledgement of God. Now, I don't mean all writers are like this, but I am certain many are. For writers, if not careful, will find themselves conforming to what is popular in order to be considered unique. And I suggest it is intellectually dishonest to view the world this way. And this intellectual dishonesty will in some way either shrink or lessen the value of their work. Because many of them deny their own continuous search for a meaning beyond themselves, which is greater than ourselves.

Also, there is a question I will ask this audience.

I simply will question how many of them, go a day, or even a moment, without wishing, and hoping, for things to turn out their way? That is, for what they themselves consider justice, or their due, to come their way.

If you placed this theory in front of them—that is, that they wish and hope (nay, pray) for things to go their way—some will castigate you for reminding them of their fallacy. Or at least contravene you by saying it has an irrelevance in literature. It is childish. But if they are childish in so spectacular a way, hoping and dreaming (praying) for their lives to change every day, and in all times of crisis, then is nothing else they think and do childish as well?

Or is everything? Most likely their lives are much more childlike than they assume. This is important in many respects, for perhaps one should not consider it a bad thing. One might remember that God asks us in the Gospel to seek Him as little children do, "become as little children."

I think this is meaningful. It is so meaningful we might become embarrassed by it. Why should we, especially those of us who are strong as oxen or as learned as Erasmus, go to anyone like "little children." The very thought can make us squirm.

But my idea is not that we don't to this, but that in point of fact we do—and that whenever we do seek Him, in whatever way, no matter how thickly veiled to us who it is we seek, we are, as He asks us to be, little children. And any hope or wish for the better of others, for our relatives or friends, or ourselves, is done in this way, like children.

Even if we do not want to be. Because of one thing—the faith we have put in our request being answered. None of us would make a request, in any way, if we did not have faith; not that it would be fulfilled, but what is more startling and important, that it could be. And to have faith is to be like a child, for faith is never determined by ourselves but by something outside of ourselves. And so we come to that Something like a child.

"Hope springs eternal," Alexander Pope writes, with some degree of universal sarcasm. And I agree with him that it does spring and is often unanswered. But neither Pope nor I, nor anyone else, can for certain tell anyone what prayer has been or hasn't been answered in our lives. Or in what way.

Truman Capote knew this only too well. Nor am I being cynical about his unfinished novel, *Answered Prayers*. I am saying he knew what he had prayed for, and how he had used what he received.

There is a Portuguese proverb that states: In many crooked ways, God makes a straight line. It is something to think about when thinking of anyone's prayers being answered or not.

I will mention once again that even an agnostic hoping for a tenure-track position will say a silent prayer to a God unknown. And in this, we are like children. Perhaps the agnostic praying is in a way much more so—more vulnerable the client, so to speak.

This is, however, an important point.

The idea of being childlike.

For this is what forms the rationale of this book—to be like children or not to be.

Just let me say that the best of us, or at least the best of us that I know, are like little children—or have a childlike quality that makes us so. I can't think of one moment where we look at someone in love and awe, where they aren't in some great respect childlike. Those who are at their best, when they are, are most often like children. We remember much about a person, and mostly what delights us about them are their childlike qualities. Gaiety always comes with those qualities of childlike innocence. Love does too. In *War and Peace*, Pierre is childlike, and so too is Natasha— so too is old Rostov, and Natasha's mother when she cuddles her. So is Tushin when he fights to protect his forgotten battery at the battle of Austerlitz. That is, at their best moments, they are childlike.

These are fine and immaculate statements by Tolstoy. When we see our loved ones acting not childishly, but childlike we realize why we love. But it is more than just realizing why we love. In fact, these qualities allow us to love both that person and ourselves, for we know that the person exhibiting these childlike qualities loves us, and we can do no less at that moment than love them. And the truth about love, as Saint Faustina said, is that "Love has only one measure, to be measureless." Yet something within our nature wants to make the child in us fail. To make us forget that we are children.

But no one can seek that Something without this character trait—to be childlike. It is a character trait that is with us all our lives. Besides this, no one I have ever met is immune from wanting and hoping in silence for something else.

All of us do hope for something better than we have now. No matter who or what we are, or how we arrived at what pinnacle we did, we are always, always dissatisfied and need assurances from Something else—Something that is beyond our own self. We need it and crave it, not because it is not there, but because too many occurrences in our lives have made us realize that it is.

We might shrink from anyone bringing this up in serious debate, or ever bringing it up ourselves in front of others, because of embarrassment and a certain civil code, which implies that religion is not only dangerous but repressive and counterproductive. That is why the tenet of the secular artist has become as absolute as medieval proclamation.

And in many respects the wonder of humanity, and of the very childlike qualities we seek in others and ourselves, has been downplayed because of this. Or I should say, more to the point, not given its due as to where it actually comes from and what it is actually seeking. The other problem with this is intellectual dishonesty, and the real danger of falling into it, to impress those with conventional views. To conform with the views of the day in order to have your views sanctified as cutting-edge views.

So this intellectual dishonesty has it roots in what I have mentioned briefly above, convention.

A contempt prior to investigation has one sole stipulation. It must be conventional. And it must conform to thought that is the prevailing thought, for it has not been investigated on its own. Once more I will say that all writers are not like this. But there are writers, and writers who are considered and celebrated, who will be like this always.

I mentioned before what Einstein said: "Christianity will never be explained away by a smart remark."

———

Something struck me while reading William Manchester's *The Last Lion*. Writing about Winston Churchill's love of a movie about the faith of a child who was taking his donkey to see the pope, in hopes it would be cured, Churchill was heard whispering, "Don't let the donkey die."

Manchester thought this childish and unsophisticated and is almost embarrassed to relate it about a man he so admires, and wants the world to admire as well. Yet most of us, in that moment, might whisper the same thing, to the same Something, with the same faith the child, who owned the sick donkey, had. I remember doing the same thing when my dog Gracie took sick years ago. And my wife, who at first did not like the dog, sat beside it tears streaming down her face. And not to understand this is to make light of ourselves. Which we can do if we forget we are children.

Is it praying for a miracle? Well, who hasn't? Many who look upon this in scorn have prayed for miracles—for cures for loved ones. Like children, I suppose. But does this mean because we do or don't, miracles do not happen? I am sure they do happen—that is, things that would not seem to be possible become so. But I am also sure that we will never know—because the real trick is that, like children, most of us do not know how things happen. And not one of us can be assured that the security and comfort we have at any moment will be guaranteed. Even for a second. And to say we are sure is a fallacy. Therefore to say that anything is certain about our role in the universe is a fallacy. Therefore to say, by extension, that we know what is miraculous and what is not is also a fallacy. A man lost in the Amazon flounders for days alone, and finally, coming to a pool in the river, decides this is where he will die. His friend searching for him in a boat is about to turn back, but tells his guide, "No, just go up to that pool and turn."

Many cynics would say this was accidental. The man who was saved might not. He might think of cynics as Oscar Wilde did, that they "know the price of everything and the value of nothing."

I might say the same thing about a little girl in the 1920s who was lost in the woods. Everyone had given up on her. But after many days she was found alive. It was an incredible feat—a miraculous one. The young child told her mother and father that fairies took care of her. That they came to her, and brought her food, and kept her safe. Ridiculous? Any rational person would say, "Yes, absolutely ridiculous." The child's parents never had the luxury of such indifference.

But what I have noticed over the last thirty years or so is not that people do not believe this. That to me is understandable. But what I find less understandable is the anger some have toward others who believe. And how much it bothers their intellectual and worldly order that someone would dare say—well, say that all life is a miracle, that Saint Augustine was in many ways absolutely right, that everything is a miracle, and that pride starts when we accept our breath and sinew as being ours. But there is something else I have thought of. Not to negate this idea of miracle means in some way that we must live for it—or because of it—and to do so means that we must change our lives; for taken to its logical conclusion, believing without doing so makes us far more illogical than Saint Francis or Saint Dominic. That their worship is understandable if we believe it is the worship of the source of creation.

"Look at how much shock and terror there is in the world and yet you dare to believe that," one said to me.

Well, he himself dared believe in the marriage of his daughter, and spent a small fortune believing in this marriage. And the wedding was in some respects like a fairy tale, and we know by experience the marriage will be many things besides.

How dare others believe what I don't—is part of the mantra that narrows us all. I have noticed it bothers lapsed Catholics more than most, and I have dealt with them more than most, because I have been good friends with some, and have been related to more. They seem incensed that since they see *untruth* in Catholicism, all others should too, and how dare they not.

Well, there might be—*untruth* for them—and I am not going to say there is not. But the subject Catholicism deals with is a very great one, a transcendent one, in both faith and piety. Going to Catholic school from an early age, and believing if I was pleasant and nice the nuns would be nice to me was about all the truth I needed for one day. Over time, I saw some feeble ambition and cronyism and I felt outside that which was preached. It was only later I began to see that I was blaming people for being people, and transferring that blame to the very hope for transcendence that these people had in their hearts. I was looking at people and blaming them for their hope and prayers even if they could not manage to live up to them. One cannot do that without in some way lessening themselves. Yes, they failed within the church, but that did not mean I did not fail outside it. And many times. And leaving it was no guarantee of having success.

Catholicism in a way asks us to live outside the temples of the world. That we see some who live in these temples telling us to do this is disturbing. But not all tell us what to do, and not all live in those temples. Again, it is a transcendent religion, and its grace is a terrible and transcendent one, and if people fail at this transcendence, should they or others not seek to try? In fact, by the very fact others still seek to try, and that some succeed, shows not only the necessity of continuing to try, but the truth of the ultimate quest.

So then if the problem is hypocrisy in Catholicism, I admit it is a known fact I do not dispute, especially with myself. Yet, as I just mentioned, for all its stupidity and blunders, at its best Catholicism refuses to give up its belief. It is this belief, a great transcendent spiritual belief, that is attacked because of people's hypocrisy. And strangely, one has little to do with the other. That is, faith passes all understanding, and as Saint Ambrose said, he did not understand so he would have faith, he had faith so he would understand. This is relevant when dealing with all sorts of issues. Hypocrisy, not the least of them. An agnostic's or an atheist's hypocrisy, as well.

Thinking of the passionate hatred Catholicism has at times received from educated people I have dealt with across the nation and beyond, I am reminded of what George Will implied in an essay back in the 1980s: Anti-Catholicism was the anti-Semitism of the intellectual, and should be viewed as such.

Yet there is something else—the idea of the world's shock and terror being a foil for our belief in miracles.

It occurs to me often enough that none of us know exclusively how what has happened or will happen is miraculous.

And we have little or no way of knowing. The idea of those who say "let reason prevail" is utterly absurd. In fact, more absurd than most religious fanatics. We do not know the reason why. And as Pascal has said, "The heart has reasons reason does not know."

Nor do we know the simplest things. When an e-mail will come or a phone will ring to change our lives. (I know that sounds prosaic and silly, for it is just an e-mail or a phone call. Still, the fact that it is unknown by us until the moment it happens and changes our lives is neither prosaic nor silly.)

When we are pointed suddenly in a new direction, many of us will believe it is not random but intended by something over which we have no control, and for our benefit because we deserve beneficence.

All of this is only speculative, but still, some aspects of it are pertinent to our lives. So really we cannot deny the life forces that direct us in unseen ways. But because they are unseen by us, it does not mean they are not known in some greater way and for a greater meaning. If we follow this unseen knowledge, we will see it not only in our life but in the lives of all we know—and all they know, and know, and so on and on.

When I began to write this section of the book, my wife and I were in Toronto. We had decided to stay in Toronto for Christmas this year. It was too long and arduous a trip back down to our home on the Miramichi. But at the last moment we decided we should come.

We visited Peggy's uncle who was ill, two nights ago. It

was a very happy two-hour visit, for he had been like a father to my wife, whose own father died when she was thirteen, and he had walked her down the aisle when she married me.

"We will see you before the new year," I said as we left.

It was the last time I was to speak to him. He died yesterday morning. Strange. But how relieved my wife was that we decided to return home.

Then there is something else. My dog, who was laying beside my feet yesterday, was killed last night. She was an old dog, sixteen years old. Blind and half deaf, she stumbled in front of a car. Certainly there was shock and misgiving over her death—I should have been here, I should have been watchful, I usually stay outside with her. But because of the circumstances of that day, she was out alone. I am sorry for it. She was with me since she was a pup. But she was sixteen, and she did die in the place we wished her to, at our home in New Brunswick. Her death was most likely painless.

The only thing I can say is we had no foreknowledge of either of these events. And I had no foreknowledge of these two events when I first began writing about people's lack of foreknowledge. These events were out of our hands not only yesterday but for all time. We had no say. Yet we were, it seems to me, in the place we had to be, without our own self-will. I know it is a simple thing, and I know you might say, "Things happen because they happen. You are making far too much of coincidence simply because it involves you."

Maybe so—but for my wife, who got to see her uncle one last time, and for my old dog that died on our homestead, what we think or do not think can no longer matter.

I feel guilty about the old dog. Not being there when I should have been. Thinking to myself about how often one betrays those who love you, even when you don't intend to. Then you must forgive yourself. And *that* in life is as hard as anything one will ever have to do. And who do I tell this to? To the memory of the dog? Do I say I wish I had been there? To stop you before you left the yard? Who am I speaking to, and what prayer am I in fact saying?

I suppose wishing things had not happened also has its place in faith. In a strange way, a very great place for us all!

Because not only do we mourn we often seek justice or revenge over things we can't control. In fact this is our greatest problem. I have lived my life where I have seen enough of violence, and I have studied power. Both the use of power and the need for revenge destroy a faith in Something greater than ourselves.

There is a terrible story but I will relate it. About a child who was beaten by her stepmother until she was bleeding internally, and then she was ordered to eat her food or be beaten again. She told her older brother she could not eat, could he please protect her. Her brother tried to and could not, and the girl was beaten and died that night. That happened forty years ago. How in God's name do we still pray that it not have happened. So are we foolish? Not really. We will always relive the moments that we know God must address.

How many of us have longed for things to have not happened, and to address that Something and ask why? Why did you allow this to happen? This is what is so difficult—the idea that if we believe, or say we believe, we in some ways must live as if we believe in a justice greater than our own.

If we do not believe in a greater justice, or greater reason, then sooner or later anything we do can be considered just. There would be no time to mourn.

Over time, you become the perpetrator you are fighting against. This is easily mocked because Nietzsche said it 140 years ago and he is not taken seriously now. Still, it is nonetheless true. If a man fights dragons, he sooner or later becomes one. But it is not only Nietzsche who has warned us against this hardness of heart. We were warned against it three thousand years ago. It would be fine to say it didn't matter that it was said three thousand years ago, if the same problems weren't so manifest today.

That is: "'Vengeance is mine,' sayeth the Lord." And we must remember this. That Cain killed Abel, and God did not kill Cain.

But what I am saying is something else besides. Very much like Cain, when we take matters into our own hands, part of us knows we are acting to spite and disobey the notion of a far greater justice, and in some ways this very spite *proves* the fact that the greater justice does exist. Cain knew it existed and we should not forget it does.

In such a strange way, our denying it proves it—at the moment we do so, we know it. That is, most revenge is done in spite of something greater than ourselves. Something God has asked us not to do. You see, we already believe it, for if we really did not believe in a greater justice, more of us would show an intemperate desire to seek justice on our own.

So when we seek this justice, we know we are seeking it in spite of a greater justice. And to do this, to manage this, we foster a hardness of heart not just against those we strike out at, but against the thing we know exists—God's Justice.

But there is another more dangerous hardness of heart, not against those who have done us wrong, but against those who have trusted and loved us, who we ourselves have injured and betrayed. In fact, as Abel trusted Cain.

This is, in fact, the real place where our unforgiving nature takes hold, and it is at times impossible to overcome. It is the continual story of Cain. So the truth of this story is continuous.

Alden Nowlan, the poet from New Brunswick, has a profound take on this. He writes in a poem that when one has commended themself for forgiving those who have done them wrong, they are ready for the sterner test, to forgive those they themselves have humiliated, cheated, and betrayed. This means we have to admit we cheated and betrayed, and it is usually done to people we do not think worthy. Why? Well, many times they loved us more than we loved them. So we, because of their love, believed we were better than they were. Since we cannot forgive ourselves we cannot forgive them.

So hardness of heart and self-righteousness are, in fact, pretty interchangeable. That is hardness of heart and self-righteousness are bedfellows—and not so strange bedfellows.

There is something about our injustice toward those we have injured that might come to haunt us sooner or later. On a personal level, that is why some of us get so dismissive of those we have harmed and make excuses for ourselves: "It was not my fault—it was his/hers" we say. Yet some part of us knows this is not true. So we buoy ourselves by saying, "All people do it. I am not the only one. I am only human."

And this idea that we are human gives us sanction to say and do that which we feel would lessen or ignoble others. But by the very fact of saying "I am human" to give ourselves licence is a convenience and, in the end, a lie we tell ourselves.

For it is the very fact of our being human that addresses the idea that a certain action we took against someone might be very wrong. So we are saying "I am human" to deny the very reason our humanity has secretly addressed this issue. If we persist in denying we are responsible, a hardness of heart sets in toward those we have harmed. This is not an esoteric principle I am preaching. It is a day-to-day struggle with our own tendencies to control those around us. Teachers have done this to children in classes, when I was in school years ago. Unthinking priests and ministers have done it as well. They have done harm to families they take no responsibility for, yet they were the ones in a position of trust.

But so do businessmen and artists, and philanthropists, too. We have all at times used those we feel free to dismiss as being not as significant as ourselves. To think this is ungoverned or sanctioned because of the absence of overt disapproval is to mask our intention and trivialize the damage of glibly using faith others put in us.

So the only way to sanction it is to applaud ourselves for doing it. At times another's faith in us makes us laugh at the faith others have put in us—excusing oneself by saying, "I cannot help it if they are so damn gullible."

And this sparks a kind of resentment that is allowed to

fester. So you become angry at those you in some way have attempted to destroy. And this becomes buoyed by self-righteousness.

"Am I my brother's keeper?" Cain asks. There are very few statements more self-righteous. But the answer is, of course, one that Cain has himself helped invent by his very act. He has patterned the crime in order to make the question one that has to be asked.

A con is at all points counting on self-deception, and more importantly, and this is the real issue, it relies upon an imitation of the virtue of faith. That's the real substance of it—that the con is almost always an imitation of faith, whether it is a faith healer or a car dealer. None of us ever overcomes the idea of using faith in our lives.

In *Huckleberry Finn*, the Duke and the Dauphin's con of the family they have claimed to be related to is buoyed at the best possible moment by the daughter, who gives into her own sense of pride by a perverse blind trust that allows the scam to continue. Her walk across the room to take sides and give the charlatans rights to the money shows this unnatural human pride, and Twain's ability to reveal how it positions itself in our lives.

But this entire scene, where the Duke and Dauphin posture as long-lost relatives of the dead father, is really a study of the falsification of faith, a distortion that rules the hearts of men and women who are continually wanting to prove they have faith in Something. Anything! It is, in fact, how every con works—we rely on mankind's need to have faith, and his search for faith allows the confidence man or woman to skewer that faith by saying they must have it, and then turning on them like a cobra to destroy it. It really is a diabolical perversity, and allows finally for the dissolution of faith.

But there is something more subtle that Twain reveals. The young woman in *Huck Finn* is an instrument of her own destruction by believing that she shares not the faith—but the con the charlatans are perpetrating against her. That is, at some point the con is revealed to the person as the antithesis of faith, and this man or woman, aware of the set-up, blindly keeps going even against their natural instincts. In fact, all of this is so subtle it must be intellectually engineered in a manner that so understands our human fragility as to allow us to argue the presence of the supernatural, or at least to debunk us as rational human beings, even if we do carry the banners of secular truth.

Our own ability to cheat others and then not be able to forgive them shows our complicity in this process of conning. And it is not just the grifters or charlatans who manage to do so. We are all charlatans at times. And our ability to cheat ourselves in the con shows the self-destructive tendency in human nature aware of an implicitness in wrongdoing that must shatter our faith in each other and our search for the Divine. It is, in a strange way, the mimicking of those we trust, even if those we trust wish to destroy not only our trust, but us as well. And the mimic is a conformist, and the con artist uses convention to achieve their purpose.

Whether in big matters or in small, if we cheat our friends, then we show not only a contempt for them but for ourselves, by trading off the innocence that comes with their trust in us as friends. And no one can tell me that this is what the better angels of our nature intended. Even if it is something slight, it might be allowed to happen, but that does not mean we have not traded on goodness for the privilege. Not only this, but our laughter at them, or our scorn for them, shows that we have conned ourselves—either in believing they were a friend or not, for no one can con others without first conning themselves.

In fact, our reasoning in this case—of cheating someone who trusts and relies upon us—is not so much different than Stalin's when he laughed after hearing that an old comrade whom he condemned to be shot had asked to see him. He laughed hysterically because he just realized how successful was the con he had pulled. But you see even more pertinent was that for the first time, he suddenly realized it was a con. Our cons come from the same arena of the soul. Oh yes, never with such evil intention, but nonetheless on the same pathway. (The mimic who hilariously revealed how this man died, begging for his life, was later shot by Stalin, begging for his own life as well.)

This is the pathway of poor Max Aitkin, Lord Beaverbrook, the man from my hometown who became minister of aircraft production in Churchill's cabinet in 1940. His life is a warning to us, not because he was such a scoundrel, for at times he wasn't. Not that he was not generous, because at times he was exceedingly so. No, he did things that were wonderful and necessary for many people, but he was also power driven, manipulative, and believed that the results of his life were determined by him alone, that there was nothing in life that he could not accomplish. This led him into an area of determinism that over time helps to defeat the soul as it promotes the man, and since he was, in his own life, trying to refute the life of his minister father, he was led into areas where promoting himself caused much pain to others. Faith, I believe, would have kept him from certain decisions that were soul-destroying, and though I give a positive view of him in my book, *Lord Beaverbrook*, and do believe that he deserves much credit, I believe his failure was ultimately one of a lack of, or a fear of, faith. This determinism is almost always a prerequisite to sin—and will over time lessen us.

He, like so many of us, did not murder, but faith is the one real insistency to keep us off that path altogether, or to keep helping us get off when we stumble on.

As Mortimer Adler says, certain actions are a difference only in degree but not in kind. And this observation is one of the most significant I have ever read, when trying to delineate man's position in the world and why he or she does the things he or she does.

One must realize that the difference in kind has nothing to do with amount, but with substance, or the reason why. The reason why is everything. We know that a woman killing a man in self-defence or to protect a child is not murder at all. Someone who blows someone's head off at a kitchen table—well, that's another matter.

The reason creates a difference in the essence of the action, and is the only way to understand the discrepancy between degree and kind.

Christ's lauding of the widow giving her last farthing while the rich Pharisees gave their allotment is of course a difference in kind. And it comes because of the reason in the giving. The self-deception the Pharisees exhibit is in evidence to Christ, and he sees it and comments on it. (The Pharisees are very aware of this deception. That is why they are so angry with Christ.) He tells them they are people who revere the prophets their own ancestors have killed, and indicates they will kill the greatest prophet by his own presence. They, of course, do not see him as a prophet. But he is saying something else. He is telling us that the con rules lives that are stingily correct, who believe they can order God to them. (Or in another way, to tell us there is no God.)

That the Pharisees are aware of this con, in my estimation, shows how they have negated the very reasons for their offerings. It is, in a way, Christ's spirit of the law, commenting on the law. The law of religion is what Lord Beaverbrook and so many others who I have come to know over the years rebelled against, but he (and others) did not search for the spirit of the law outside his own determinism. What Christ is speaking of, and concerned about, is the con that disables people's trust in the religious spirit, which men and women so desperately need, and allows this determinism to not only rule but to exploit ourselves, so people decry not only the religious law but the spirit of the law.

What we have to realize here is that the religious self-con is condemned by Christ as easily as by Christopher Hitchens. Hitchens is a brilliant man, and in his book refuting God's existence he mocks the self-con. He hates the fanatical religious appeal without realizing that so many believers hate it as well—that there is something truly beatific about faith that ennobles the spirit and is useless to argue about. I believe I have met one true saint in my life—I believe she would never argue with anything any agnostic or atheist said. To her, there would be no point at all.

Both Christ and Hitchens, and, in a more trifling way, the comedian Bill Maher, hate the religious self-con. Yet they do so for very different reasons, and their condemnation is in itself a difference in kind. Christ condemns the posture of faith because it has nothing really to do with faith—faith is something he wants all men and women to experience, and dies for them to do so.

Hitchens and Maher condemn the con for a far narrower reason. Both see faith as the con itself, and they cannot equate the profound difference between the two.

And that, in a way, is the argument of this book, that here is the vast difference—the untold incalculable difference between the true wealth of that woman and the wealth of the Sadducees and Pharisees. If there is no difference, then it will not matter the answer to this question, which is, after two thousand years, the same question: Who in fact, morally and spiritually, would we rather be?

This is a question I posed once before. It comes from Operation Barbarossa launched by Hitler against Stalin in June of 1941. I spoke about the nihilistic symptom of thinking man's ingenuity and grasp of invention makes us superior to superstition and faith. And recounted an incident where a tiger tank, hatch opened, is roaring through a village with the young German tank driver laughing hilariously at a poor peasant woman in front of him, trying to pick up her hens to save them from being run over. Over half a century later this still speaks to us, as a betrayal of humanity that invention never solved. And the question remains: Who in fact would we rather be?

But what allows this self-con when we manage to exploit the faith of others? What allows this is in fact the greatest thing a modern person has: cynicism. The cynicism of the tiger tank officer on the first day of Operation Barbarossa.

"A cynic knows the price of everything and the value of nothing."

A friend of mine fought for a number of years to get his compensation for having fallen while working as a boiler-maker in Saint John, a fall that partially disabled him. Finally, he received this money. No sooner had he, when an "old friend" dropped by with a "certain" business proposal. My friend, who was no businessman, and had always looked up to this man, went into partnership, giving his compensation literally away. In a month he was broke. His friend walked away, shaking his head at what had happened, and, of course, disappointed in him.

We are often like the Sadducees and Pharisees in the marketplace. Wisdom is not used to discover the inner spirit of man but to disavow it, and to mock those who have it or try to find it. And all it takes to do this is power. My friend, who lived all his life without much and lost his compensation, has no power. But in the end he will be happier than the man who took it from him.

That I guarantee.

Which brings me back to my initial topic of miracle and my hope in it, and my feeling that miracle can change hardness of heart.

"Do not fear," Christ tells us, "for I have overcome the world."

And he is speaking here to my friend who has lost his compensation, as much as anyone else.

There is something so pure in those words that only the deepest of cynics would not recognize its truth, or, at the very least, not hope that in some way it was true. (The woman with her hens, if she lives, will realize this truth—but more importantly, so will the tank driver himself, no later than 1944.)

In my lifetime I have had certain, if few, remarkable instances of the presence of God. From my very earliest days, I recognized this presence now and again. Other times, I am sure I dismissed it. These instances most often came in ways I least expected from the time I was a child. I will simply relate them, not as miraculous events as much as incidents that left a profound impression. Make of them what you will.

There is a mall in West Saint John, down near the highway, that is open at noon on Sundays. I went there once in February to sign some books and arrived when the shops were closed, the parking lot empty. The main door was open so I went in to wait, and sat on a dark bench in the main foyer. The walls were empty, the stalls barren, the air was darkened with only winter light, and now and again there was the sound of the automated voice recordings over the games of chance that were peppered here and there throughout the mall: "You too can be a winner," they said with a kind of troubling robotic merriment.

Now and again there was a sound, like the sound of footfall on a dark November street, the shuffling and clanking of something I could not see. But then, when I least expected it, a woman passed me, and I recognized her. She was a woman who had at one time taken care of my oldest child when he was two and three years old. She would come in the mornings, when my wife went to work, so I could go into the study to write. She would pull John on an old wagon across the back field to the little fort they had made, with his blanket and picnic lunch. Just as all kind-hearted people do with children. She was overweight and hadn't much in her life. Her children were her life, in fact, and she hoped so much for them. I had not seen her in fifteen years.

I called her name and she looked up at me. Her eyes were filled with an indescribable sorrow, and I was not only shocked but, for the first time in a long time, I felt suddenly that I had not done right by humanity. And she was at that moment there to tell me so—and that I did not go to that mall to sign a few unimportant books, but that I was sent there by that Something to show me what I had missed. That is, that if I had tried to put these feelings into my books, I had missed them in my life. That I paid her money but not paid attention, as she spoke hopefully about her own life, and took care of my child, who she loved. And that she had loved my child as I had. And that she had deserved much better from me, because for a short while I had been her hope. I do not know why this feeling came over me, and was so overwhelming. But in part it was because of where we were. The mall, which is like the church of today, that calls to all of us. So it was in this church that we met. If I had not been there, I would not have received this message—in a strange way a blessing. I do not think that I have ever in my life felt stronger the presence of God than at that moment. It does sound ridiculous, but is nonetheless so.

The presence of God was between her and I, and it was almost palpable. It was as if this presence was telling me to hold her. It was timeless, and her moving slowly along our back fence with my child became seared in my heart as I stood there.

What had happened to her? When we left for Toronto, years had passed, and her soul somehow died, as did her hope. In those days with my child, there was a hope that things would be okay, and I did not know how urgent it was for her to earn that bit of money, and to talk with me a few minutes a day. It was my obligation to know and I had not. God was telling me this now.

She looked frightened of me, and I did not want her to be—and I realized she was sorrow-filled, completely.

"Where is your husband," I asked?

"He is away more than he is home."

"Where are your children?"

"They are gone, grown up now."

I did not ask why she was walking through the mall, where the redundant voices kept saying: "You too can be a winner."

But I had to say something. I wanted to say more. I wanted for some reason, and I have never felt this more strongly, to ask forgiveness. I told her the boy she had held had grown up now and was a man. She nodded, again her eyes looked away.

"Yes, he must be getting big now." She smiled. She told me she had to go, that if she kept her husband waiting, he would be mad.

"God loves you," I said. It was the only thing I could think to say.

"Thank you," she said.

And she turned and hobbled to the door.

Never was I so sure that I was meant to meet her, at that moment, and that when I said, "God loves you," I was meant to tell her that. Perhaps to let her know that at that moment, in a mall, closed up and at the end of the earth, God loved her more than He loved me.

Frederick Buechner speaks about man never being able to trust God after they realize He was born in a stable. This tells us that God's awful power and majesty not only can but will appear in the most inauspicious of places. I knew, in this darkness of a midday empty mall, how utterly, utterly true and how terribly humble and imposing God's love really is. That was what was so startling. The terrible beauty and love in that moment, out of nothing at all. It was strangely awesome.

But that lady is gone now, and I will probably never see her again.

There is a line in a novel I remember, written by a writer from Trinidad who I read some years ago: "I have just betrayed my brother." Seeing her that day, I realized later, tears in my eyes, this is what all of us have done.

———

I was four years old. And on those days, long ago, my mother was often ill. My two older siblings were in school, and I was free, after kindergarten, to wander here and there—to cross that street where I had been driven over by a car, and make my way up the hill toward Station Street, where I could visit Mrs. Ronan who would give me a cookie. I did this faithfully, like a mouse hooked on sugar water. The days in May were wonderful then, the trees leafing after winter, and everything smelling of mud and warmth. Life in abundance, so to speak. A great time to be a child.

Often, as I tottered up Jane Street, a woman in the house next to Mrs. Ronan's watched my journey as I made my way. I remember she had dark hair, and a thin face, and how she held her fingers against the buttons of her print dress when she came out to me one sunny afternoon. She ran out to me, actually, as if I was a mailman who had forgotten to give her important mail. Like a child.

"Hello, can I speak with you just a second?"

The sun shone on those white delicate fingers, and I remember them as if it was yesterday. This would have been about fifty-five years ago. She was a young mother who had a baby who was dying of a brain tumour. And he would die in the next few weeks. And she had come out to that sidewalk, on those days gone far away, to ask me for my help. Really, she asked me in desperate hope, why I was like I was. My affliction gave her hope, a tremendous hope she hadn't had in months. She had hope that my condition meant that I too had once been like her child, but had succeeded by some miraculous means to live. Life is what she was asking God for, through me. And I was the walking, talking little miracle.

I stood there, all two feet of me, and tried to help her.

Was I sick like her child? Did I remember? Of course, I said, I was very sick, too. Did the doctor perform an operation that made me well? I was almost sure he had—that is, like most children with grown-ups, I gauged what it was she wanted to hear and said it. Where was this operation performed? In a city, I was sure.

It was strange to me that hobbling about as I did, tripping over everything, gave someone hope. But it did, unquestionably. Her husband came out and called her back, as if she had disobeyed him. And she turned round to see him and then looked back at me, as if I could in some way keep her from something just a moment longer. Then she turned away.

I know as she turned to walk back she was not as hopeful as when she ran to see me. By the time I got home that afternoon, my mother had received a call from her husband, and strangely my mother asked me not to go up there again for awhile. So I did not go.

They were waiting for her child to die, and they did not want her to hope because of me. But, you see, I was as smart as they were. I knew the woman had no hope—she latched on to me for it. And it was a comfort to her. So I should have been allowed to see her. For if she really wanted to know the truth, she would have sought it elsewhere. She did not come to me for truth, but for hope. She did not want the "truth" as they understood it, she wanted me to tell her she still had hope of a greater truth. And she had faith that I would tell her that she still had hope, because grown-ups—people like her husband and my parents—no longer gave that to her. So she had returned to being a child. A little girl no older than I was.

It was a pact between her and I, just for a little moment, that she could believe in miracles. I allowed her that. Did the miracle come? That is the question, isn't it? Well, looking back, the chance that a woman of twenty-four would speak to a child of four years of age, hoping that he had wisdom to tell her something, is in itself something of a miracle of faith. That is the true miracle. She was in the end searching, blindly perhaps, in need of charity.

In some way, she knew, too, that in order for her to have faith, she must let go of this kind of hope and be resolved to embrace another. A hope of a different kind—of faith in a meaning beyond her, for her child and herself. And I am not suggesting smugly that this came from meeting me, or that it should come because she lost a child. In the end, this was the only place the hope pointed to—it pointed down the sunny rocky sidewalk to faith.

In effect, both her husband and my mother were each in their way exhibiting a charity, too. It seemed cold but, in the end, perhaps it was not at all.

Sometime in the summer, after her child died, they moved away. I do not know what happened in her life. I was never to see her again. Perhaps over time she forgot me, I do not know. I know I could never forget her. I would like to talk to her even now—and if alive she would be approaching her eightieth year. Yet that child of hers remained forever an infant, and in so many respects she and I have never aged at all.

———

My mother died in Montreal, January 13, 1978. I had gone on December 23, when she was still in hospital in Fredericton, to a gift shop and bought her one of the Royal Doulton figurines she had collected for years. I never gave it to her—waiting, as I told Peg, for when she came home, even though we knew that was probably not going to happen. She was transferred to Montreal and died on January 13 in the Royal Victoria, where my grandfather had died of diabetes on October 17, 1924.

Those days are pretty much a blur. But there is one thing I remember that seems pretty inconsequential. The first song I heard after getting back to New Brunswick was Paul Simon's "Mother and Child Reunion."

Strange enough, but easily explainable. After 1978, my wife and I drifted here and there. We were at odds and ends within our lives. Never knowing where we would settle, and finding where we did settle never satisfactory. I suppose being a writer had something to do with it. Having little money was another reason. Having a career that seemed to be going nowhere was part of it as well. From Newcastle, we went back to Fredericton for a time, and then to Saint John, and then on to Toronto. It was in January 1998, when I was trying to get my study into shape, in the basement of our first house. I was opening boxes of books with some amount of weary duty. I opened one more and then another, and finally came to the last.

Sitting inside this box was a toy wrapped in plastic. I picked it up and looked at it. Not sure what it was, I unwrapped it, discovering the little figurine. I had not thought of it in years, really—did not even know where it came from. It had been packed away with so many other things. That day was January 13, 1998—the twenty-year anniversary of my mother's death. It was only then that I realized this. You could say a lot of things. You could say it was complete coincidence. Or you could say she was handing it back to me, to keep it for her. And that her death in the past and mine in the future were, in the words of Paul Simon's song, "only a motion away."

My grandmother was a widow at the age of thirty. She operated a theatre in our little town of Newcastle. There were some people who were interested in putting her out of business, and one group persuaded the local bank manager, who owed them a favour on a gambling debt, to foreclose on her mortgage. This was devastating to her. Though she had grown up in tough circumstances, she did not know that business people were actually willing to treat someone like this. She found it out, as they say, the hard way.

She said one thing as she left the bank that day in 1928: "You cannot injure people in this way without it coming back on you. I hope you know that."

The bank manager did not seem to consider it. My grandmother, Janie, went to people she knew, who had no money, and then finally to a stranger, who did. He was a lumber baron in our area, and she boldly knocked on his door—the first Protestant door she ever knocked on, she told us. She told him how much money she needed—a few thousand, I think, which was a great amount to her.

"Sure, Janie," he said. "I'll loan you the money."

She was able to pay off her mortgage, which surprised her rivals. And later on in the year she was able to travel to Montreal and get a monopoly on talking pictures, which everyone thought to be a passing phase. She put the other theatres out of business, and easily paid off the debt to the lumber baron.

Late that next year, her opposition tried to blow up her theatre, but the dynamite was found. She became over time fairly wealthy as well as reclusive. She mistrusted many and had an unhappy life. It was in 1952 that she received a surprise call from the widow of the bank manager. He had died in the pauper's home, and his widow did not have the money to pay for the funeral. Janie was the only working woman she knew, and so she approached her.

"Of course," my grandmother said. "Bury your husband properly and send the bill to me."

I wrote a novel, *River of the Brokenhearted*, which was in some ways about my grandmother. I was going to include the scene where she warned the bank manager that everything was sooner or later answered. I mentioned it to my editor and both of us felt that no one would believe it, because some things that happen in the world don't happen in fiction.

In 1978, the year my mother died, an elderly man entered the tavern where I drank almost every day. He came in and sat down beside me.

"I want to buy you a drink," he said.

"Sure," I replied. "And then I'll buy you one."

"No," he said. "I don't drink any more."

So he bought me a drink and then looked at me a moment and said, "You're Janie's boy?"

"No," I answered. "I am Janie's grandson."

"Oh well, how time goes," he answered.

And we spoke about how time goes, and how it always seems we do not do those things we are wanting or supposed to do in our lives, and then he got up, shook my hand, and teetered away.

My friend, who was working the bar at the time, came over and said, "Do you know who that is?"

"No, I have no idea."

"He was one of the men hired to blow up your grandmother's theatre in 1928."

After all this time he had come back to say he was sorry—to the son, because the mother was dead, and found the grandson instead. It had been with him all this time. To him, it may have only been a second passed. And yet, in some way, it all worked out.

My wife's cousin had Down's syndrome and was one of the least. He was supposed to live no longer than ten years, however he lived until he was thirty-one. I do not know if any of you know a Down's syndrome child—they are magnificent ambassadors of unconditional love. Wayne lived until he was thirty-one, and I remember those times I met him as the granting of grace, and felt his exuberance for living.

He gave this grace to everyone who knew him for as long as he could. He would have given it to Stalin in a second. No matter what his own condition was, when he saw anyone, his face would brighten into a huge smile, accepting of all that was.

When he was dying, his mother was there in the room with him. He was quiet for quite a long time, and then suddenly he looked at her, saying, "Mom, everyone is here."

"Who is here?" she asked, startled.

"They are all here and want me to tell you that they have come to take me to heaven."

He named relatives of his he could never have known, some who had died years before he was born. Then he simply blessed himself, closed his eyes, and went to sleep.

My wife and I had just moved to Toronto a year or so before, and my wife had taken our youngest child, Anton, to a summer playschool. One day, in midsummer, my wife received a call from a woman, who had just emigrated from Kosovo.

"I met you at playschool. I have a daughter, Michelle," she said.

"Oh yes, of course."

"I wonder if you could do me a favour."

"Yes," Peggy said.

"Well, I wonder if you could take care of my child. The doctors say I need an operation, and I know no one else in Canada but you."

And this is how we came to be godparents of Michelle, and friends with her mother and her father. Anila was, in fact, very ill, with a brain tumour. She was twenty-eight years of age, beautiful, and had just emigrated to Canada, looking for a better life than the one she had left behind. She had a degree in mathematics but could not teach here, and so she worked at a grocery store. George worked at night in a hotel. And now this life of hope in Canada looked far, far away from anything she knew.

We helped take care of Michelle for a long time, and grew to love her very much. But Anila's treatment did not go well. After the operation, when she told us confidently that they were able to get 95 per cent, I knew it was a percentage arrived at to give her hope in a hopeless situation. As she went downhill, I realized as I always did with people who are dying that there are three stages. Hope, hope the treatment is wrong and that another is needed, and when realizing hope is gone, faith that it must be God's will. It is not easy—not for her, who was so brave and so determined, and not for us, who watched as her seizures became more frequent, or for her husband, who realized long before she did that she was dying.

She wanted her child to become Catholic since her child did go to the Catholic school, and asked us to be godparents.

They needed the name of a Catholic saint to add to Michelle's name if she was about to be baptized—the standard devotion in Catholic law—and Anila asked me what name could we give her.

I thought of two Catholic saints, both important to me, Saint Joan of Arc and Saint Bernadette, and asked her if she could make Michelle's middle name Bernadette.

Anila liked this very much. And so she did.

No treatment worked, and they moved to London, Ontario, because George had a job there, and there was a fine hospital. But we did not see her again.

Then at the end, when she was to fly with her daughter and husband back to Albania to die, she had her husband phone us to say goodbye. She wouldn't allow us to come to the airport to see her. Her features had changed so much that she wanted us only to remember what she had been like, that beautiful young woman so filled with hope and dreams for a child who would grow up now without her. So brave that she had taken a chance to phone a complete stranger from another culture and ask for help with a little girl she did not want to leave alone.

My wife was very upset she couldn't go to the airport, for she wanted to embrace her. But she never got the chance. Anila died on Christmas Day, 2004, at the age of thirty-one.

It was in the middle of summer, a few years later, and I happened to be in town. George telephoned and said he was in Toronto with Michelle and his mother, and could they drop over.

"Of course," I said, delighted. I was only in town for two days, and happy our paths would meet. I was only sad that Peggy and Anton were not here as well, but at our house in New Brunswick.

I finished the day—I had to see my publisher and do an interview about my friend Alistair MacLeod, and came back to the house an hour or so before they arrived. I took a shower, and was in the bedroom, standing near an old book-shelf. I bent over to straighten up some books that were lopsided and then saw something sticking out of one of them. I lifted it out of the book.

It was a picture of Michelle and her mother Anila, when they had first arrived at our house. Sitting side by side on a loveseat in the living room, smiling at the camera. I had completely forgotten the picture even existed, but I knew in an instant Anila intended it to be given to her daughter, and she had made sure I found it. She made sure George telephoned and that I would be here. For me, there can be no other explanation, and never will be. To say it is all coincidence is as unrealistic as to determine ten thousand angels on the head of a pin. I could have easily gone another two years without finding it.

Anila wanted Michelle to have this picture so she would know. That night I told Michelle that this picture was a gift directly from her mother, and had almost nothing whatsoever to do with me. She also wanted Peggy to remember how she was once, radiant and alive and wonderful and full of love, and to know that she is that way now.

Friends of ours adopted a child. We became very close both to them and to the boy. The couple pondered over a name and finally decided to call him Luke, which seemed a slightly strange decision to some of their friends. A month or so later they received a letter from the birth mother, who was living in Australia. She asked them to love her child—which they did, of course, because he was now their own. She asked them to tell him something about Australia, which they would do. She asked them—and they had no prior knowledge of this—to name him Luke.

I remember a friend reading from a book he wrote about the self-interest of childless people who adopted from a poor single mother. For a day or two it made me slightly ashamed that my wife and I had adopted.

For a time, I was bothered by the insistence of some kind of collusion in adoption that his reading suggested, and felt, because of this, less in my children's eyes—something I had never felt before. I know it is silly to make too much of it, but I was bothered nonetheless.

But then one day, last year, I suddenly realized how foolish I was to think this, for Something reminded me in a moment of reflection: "You yourselves have decided nothing—nothing at all. Your lives are as all others in one tremendous regard— your lack of control over what would or could happen." So I began to reflect on how our children came to be with us.

Just as in the naming of Luke or the finding of a picture, I do not think we had a choice. Our first child was adopted because we were sidetracked to go to Saint John instead of moving to Toronto. And by that time both of us had given up on the idea of ever having children. We were on our way to Toronto, and drove to Saint John to say goodbye to my brother and nieces, when my brother suddenly convinced us to buy a house in Saint John

We did this because we were at loose ends, with no thought of having a fixed place to stay. Most of our lives we have had no fixed place. But it was because of this sudden and seemingly impulsive decision that gave us our own house that we were able to adopt our first child, which we would never have done if we had phoned to say goodbye as we had intended, instead of driving down.

We were in Saint John only four or five months when a phone call came out of nowhere one day, and suddenly our first child came into our life.

We are far from perfect parents. But I will guarantee my friend this—there were no other parents in the world our first child was meant to have. And, mistakes aside, no one could love him even an eighth as much as we do, ever at all!

I suppose our second child is even more proof that this condition, where we do not know, and cannot decide, is a true and absolute condition that implores us to rely on faith, even if it is so often in hindsight.

We went to Spain in 1994, intending to stay from November through until May or June.

Back in Saint John, without us knowing anything about it, in January 1995, a woman we had never before met phoned a mutual friend to tell him that she was pregnant and wanted to put her child up for private adoption. She asked if he knew anyone who might want to adopt her baby. He mentioned our names instantly, and she asked if she could meet us. He told her we were in Spain for the year. She felt she would be too far along in her pregnancy by the time we came home and decided she must find another couple to make sure the child would have a home.

But then something unusual happened.

The exact same day, my wife received a call from her sister-in-law that her mother had taken seriously ill. So that night we decided to come home, and flew back to Canada the next evening.

A day after our return, I learned that Rick Trethewey was reading in Saint John and so I went. At this gathering I met my friend who this woman had phoned. Startled that

I was back, he told me about a young woman who wanted to contact me.

"Sure," I said. "What about?"

But my friend would not say.

"She will have to tell you," he said.

Thinking it was about writing a book, I said sure, and she contacted us the next day. She asked Peggy and I to visit her. We did.

At that meeting, she told us she was pregnant and was unable to care for the child, and wondered if we might be able to adopt it.

"Absolutely," we said.

"Even if it is afflicted?"

"Without question."

She told us she had decided against us just two days ago because she didn't think we would get back from Spain in time.

So we began the process of adoption.

After a few weeks, Peggy's mother recovered and we travelled back to Spain for another three months. Our second child was born in October, and we were present at his birth.

These are the stories I have to offer. God either wills or allows, and nothing in the world can change it.

Even to those of us who many times pretend it is a lie, for many times it is hard to believe it is true. But I know from experience it was not God that lied.

These are stories that happened not in extraordinary places but in the most ordinary of ways. They happened not in some small moment to someone who is easily gulled but to a host of people I know and love.

I suppose the only way one could stop this mystery and miracle is by convention—for the conventional will always say these things did not happen to protect the conventional mind. But I am here to affirm that they did happen, and therefore could not, not happen.

I suppose it was murder that led me to this thinking. That is, that murder is the trajectory of humanity and faith is the one antidote, or the actual turning away from the exalting of the self. Slowly I came to believe that a loss of humility was a projection toward sin, and ultimately each one of us wishes to complete sin by committing murder. A strange thought, but nonetheless I think one that might be argued. Perhaps what I am thinking is that there are always many more ways than one to murder. Perhaps I am thinking that all sin strives to become the ultimate one.

Of late, I have been thinking much more about this. Faith in others telling us what we should or should not do even to the point of killing allows us to mimic and become more like others want us to be. But faith in God helps us diminish the mimic inside us, and this alone helps us prevent murder. As René Girard has said about the mimic, Christ knew that no one would throw the first stone, but that everyone would throw the second.

In my life I have had those who wanted me dead—and at one time sent their young cousins to my house, to either rob or kill, I am not sure. Nor does it matter. It was at night, I had been drinking in a bar downtown, and came home. Later I heard them at the side door trying to get in.

I knew who they were. But as I came downstairs I knew they were frightened, and they ran. But that it did not happen is less the accident of good fortune than one might assume. Certain things were meant to happen in my life and did, and certain things disallowed.

I have seen enough violence in my life to know this is true. And to know, as Buckminster Fuller once said, "God does not make mistakes."

I also believe that all of us, even those who are atheists, seek God—or at the very least not one of us would be unhappy if God appeared and told us that the universe was actually His creation. Oh, we might put Him on trial for making it so hard, and get angry at Him, too, but we would be very happy that He is here.

Well, He is.

From my first novel, where the characters were truants of the church, God was still sought, even if it was privately and even if it was in nature. This is a youthful exercise and that is why it is in my first and second novels—seeking God in nature. I do not intend to make light of it, for there is nothing wrong with it, as far as it goes.

Most First Nations tribes never saw nature as God. They knew God spoke to them, in or through nature. In the Micmac custom, a young man went into the woods until God spoke to him. But it was not nature that spoke, it was Goosecap—that is, God. Nature is, in so many ways, far different in its terror and true reality than what people who seek it wish to worship, which puts us outside that which we seek, something we do not intend. Any nudist tells us this without saying a word.

That is not such a frivolous observation as it might seem. Now nature seems to us to be at the breaking-point, and many have deified it because of this. And yet many have not spent a night or a day in the deep woods. And while we deify nature, we live life in cities that have slaughtered millions of plants and animals, and are blind to this facet of our own responsibility. It is always those terrible loggers or hunters. This is the kind of safe moralization that some have come to accept and assimilate as virtue. Almost, as faith.

I know there is some good reason to condemn organized religion. But I know also that some of this observance to nature is cant, and fairly convenient. That might sound smug but it is not meant to be. For I have seen the smugness of back-to-the-landers, who were narrow to any idea of God or duty. And in a way that's why they were back-to-the-landers. They searched for equality by embracing nature and cutting themselves off from everyone they deemed to be unequal. This search for peace and equality coming on the backs of others you deem unequal is the main obstacle to both equality and peace.

People who have disagreed with my work have often failed to bring up the quest for God as the real problem for them in a novel that professes to be modern, and to be seeking liberty.

Nor do I mind that they are upset or displeased—but I will let them know why I think they are.

The problem for some—well, for many, even many of my friends—is their belief that one cannot be seeking liberty and God at the same time. It is in bad taste, it is an unbelievable hypothesis and poor physics. Especially from a hypocrite such as I, who many have seen at my worst—which is not very nice.

Besides, the idea of religion having anything to do with freedom is both ignorant and patriarchal. (This is more important to some than they would admit—patriarchal.) But my contention is that liberty cannot be had without the other, God. That the whole premise of life is to seek God, in order to realize freedom. And that the cynicism that is sometimes afforded the search, and the mask of irony that dissects the so-called illusion is, in fact, a way to defeat freedom.

And that even books which do not profess this (and some of my books do not) have at their core this search.

"But you are the last that should say this—for no one is more hypocritical," some would say, and I could say the same about myself very easily. Yes, it is ironic in a way. But as Rilke has said, at the very crux of the matter there is no irony. And I would continue on by quoting Robert Browning:

"Ah, but a man's reach should exceed his grasp, or what's a heaven for?"

In fact, that is both Sydney's and Lyle's quest in *Mercy Among the Children*—their reach does exceed their grasp in very different ways. But this reach, in a way, is accomplished in the novel by two of the least of God's children, Sydney's wife, Elly, and their son Percy.

Then there is another line from an old folk song that the poet Fred Cogswell once said sums up all of man's hopes and dreams: "Over these prison walls I would fly." This is what both Sydney and Lyle try to do, throughout the book.

It is what we all do every breathing day. It is what I did, in Newcastle, when I worked at Sobeys, and later in the woods, and later at the mines. I would continually tell myself that one day I would be free. Over time I became aware of what some prisoners in labour camps in the Soviet Union did (although I know my life was certainly not as harsh)— the way to be free is to be morally or spiritually free. The way to be a prisoner is to be morally a prisoner. Once this becomes apparent, freedom means something more, and less, that is, physically a prisoner, morally not so much.

Man is continually trying to fly over them, the prison walls, and keeping the faith, by hoping that he can fly. And no one can deny this, about himself or anyone else.

The prison walls are I am convinced maintained by something many of us says does not exist, sin. I have argued the existence of sin, with myself, as well as others, and have wondered how this limits freedom. For my novels have always been concerned with freedom. I suppose most novels are. It is not a big thing. I don't mean it to be. Still it is, and was, and will be freedom against one thing, which, of course, is in all relative terms, unattainable. The best of my characters seek freedom *from* sin. That's what the characters in my novels, since *The Coming of Winter*, have always been confronted with. They are plagued by sin—sinning themselves and being more sinned against than sinning.

(Just like the characters in most of the novels I admire, even if it is stated or not, and even if the problems are delineated as sin or not. For Faulkner and Hemingway, the sin is cowardice and deceit. Neither may think of God in the same way as the other does, but their work is a testament to what they think of as sin.)

As much as Hester Prynne's scarlet letter, though for most of my characters more deserved, the presence of sin runs throughout my novels. Oh, not gauging unforgivable sins—though some are pretty harsh—I don't think any sin is unforgivable. Most often, in my books, sin is seen in the form of self-righteous attitudes against my main characters, or in certain ways their own self-righteousness. And, in many of my books, this leads the characters off the beaten path, for better or worse.

After a time sin becomes more self-seeking. It seeks and will seek its own kind. It will do so just by the process of elimination, for we tend to eliminate those around us who do not any longer fit with ourselves. So if one becomes addicted to cocaine, as one of my closest friends has, then the rationale is to seek others who look upon this addiction as normal. None of this is complicated, but it is self-seeking. And self-seeking sin left unabated seeks to become the one ultimate sin—murder.

It was murder that finally made me realize this is what my characters had always sought freedom from. For there is only one great sin—and all other sins seek it. All sins seek one great sin. And it is this: murder. Just like those minions of Stalin had learned to do. We are all mimics, as René Girard elaborates, and we mimic those who are more powerful. And power never seeks liberty for those it controls. It only seeks control, and this control leads to sin. Anyone who reads Machiavelli knows this to be true, and Machiavelli stipulates that the way to keep this control is by instilling fear in others.

The one thing that changes this or can combat it is Faith in God. I really do not believe anything in our makeup can combat the idea of murder more than faith. (To say that the Grand Inquisitor in *The Brothers Karamazov* murders is right, but to declare faith failed because of this, is to miss what Faith in God is—and what Dostoyevsky's argument is.)

In the course of any of my novels this is what the characters are trying to resolve. In many respects my characters are trying to decide whether or not murder is justified. It is what plagues Seaweed in *Road to the Stilt House*. And Lyle in *Mercy Among the Children*. It presents itself as the only way to be saved for Alex Chapman and Leo Bourque in *The Lost Highway*. And in all of these books the one out—and this is not a great comfort to the modern man (this is why my work is considered depressing or, what is even more untrue, my characters unlikeable)—is faith. I never started out to write this. Hell, I would be the last person to start out writing this! There wasn't a writer in the country any wilder than I was at twenty-four. And my wife and family paid for it. But, by logic, it seemed that only faith could save the desperate. And that most often the desperate are those without hope, and those who have faced great violence and sin. Just as many of my characters face. And by thirty-one, I was as desperate as any.

I guess that's why Stalin opened the churches.

But there is something else—the possibility that I might commit what I considered to be a justified murder. I had lived in a place where to take a life was considered by many I drank with to be special and significant and brave. Or, at the very least, to be understood. That may sound trite, but it is not. Nor did everyone think this, or think it always, but that some did was enough.

And there were people, at one time, that I might well have wanted dead, for they had seriously threatened me and my loved ones. That murder was considered to be the final liberty, that some people actually cheered, made me finally realize what it was my work was trying to say to me. Faith would save people—not from being murdered, but faith would save me from murdering someone else. And faith would save others from murder as well. For it is the option of sin, to commit sin and to regard sin as glamorous, that will attract us always. The absolute cynical view of Machiavelli proves this. Not only in a bar where the tough boys sit planning to raise hell by burning down a lumberyard, but in the common room where whiskered boys plan deceit and malevolence. Alex Chapman, in *The Lost Highway*, is lost long before he meets Poppy Bourque that night. And I have known more than a few Alex Chapmans in my life.

The act of murder allows you, through the disregard of others, to become heroic in the most conventional of ways. Now anyone reading this will immediately say this seldom leads to murder, and I will say that in most ways they are right. And there are instances when a good time does lead to a good barroom brawl, or raising hell, which in the end is more entertaining than harmful. And I will say, sure, again they are right. And the sowing of wild oats? Yes, that is right. Yet in a very few ways they are not right, for there are numerous pathways to the act of murder. And murder is a kind of death, slow or fast. To shoot someone in cold blood is murder, to take someone innocent and destroy him/her as I have seen conniving men of wealth do to the ignorant poor, or to take someone's best and trample it, is a kind of murder that might not show up in any court of law, but somewhere and somehow it is being recorded. So often the acts that aren't prosecuted are the ones that are as deadly. The impregnating of a young woman you do not care for and then rebuke, prevalent when I was a young man, is a kind of murder, too.

Philosophy became remarkably simple once I discovered this. That is, that killing was the sin that all other sin was attempting to be. The bully sin that all other little bully sins wished to emulate on a daily basis. And they did and do emulate it. I have seen enough of the world to know that.

But let us look at the idea of the great sins. Ingratitude is the greatest sin to David Hume, while betrayal is to Dante. So if we look at murder as something that attempts to crush one's spirit, then Hume and Dante are correct. And there are 1000, 1000 occasions where they are. Herb Curtis says in the second book of his own Miramichi trilogy that one character believes that adultery was the same as murder. So if we let sin grow enough without thinking that it matters, it will become easier and easier to take a life. Or to betray and show ingratitude in a way that compliments how Hume or Dante think. This is the danger we face, especially if we start to believe in revenge more than we believe in sin. Or believe that revenge is a positive virtue. Now I know that all or most of us have liked to or said we would, and never do. But to commit a crime or even murder because so-and-so has harmed you is in some way to rationalize one wrongdoing as sin and the other as justified. You can't do so if there is no sin, for if that is the case, the other did no wrong. If there is no wrong, then no reason for you or I to murder. If there is wrong, no matter if deeply wronged, the greatest wrong is murder, so you defeat yourself by committing it. But often it is the wrong in yourself that promotes murder.

The idea that Cain killed Abel because of his own failure is a problem most of us face in our lives. It is something in our own makeup that first disowned us, allowing us to cheat ourselves.

If we do not believe in personal responsibility, we then have less of a chance in recognizing the personality of sin.

I certainly knew how the disengagement of personal responsibility worked the time I met a bicycle messenger the day after 9/11. He seemed delighted at what had happened. I do not need to agree with American foreign policy to be disheartened by his reaction.

His glee toward this catastrophic event, which he felt to be justifiable, has bothered me ever since.

The bicycle messenger was one of many I met in Canada who allowed themselves the applauding of the 9/11 event, as if they were allowed by proxy to be a part of the conspiracy. (There were millions of Canadians, of course, who did not.)

"Yes, it is terrible," he said. "But this is the result of terrible U.S. foreign policy." Then he added, "But no one in Canada will say so, because we are far too conservative and conditioned."

But I knew this was not true at all. Many people in Canada couldn't wait to say this, and he was saying what many people his age were. (People in the United States and France and elsewhere were saying this, too.) From all parts of Canada, and on many university campuses, some were saying this very thing.

I said to my young bicycle messenger friend, "That's disingenuous. It was an evil act."

"Oh, don't be ridiculous." He smiled at the old man he spoke to. "There is no such thing as evil."

(Yet I am not sure he would have said this about U.S. foreign policy.)

We did not examine the word "disingenuous" and off he went. But I was not talking about the act being disingenuous. I was speaking of the act as being evil, and his reaction to it as being disingenuous, and fairly convenient, and if this is all it takes to be gulled into thinking that murder is brave and noble, one must not be so sure evil does not exist.

That is, though he might think I am very wrong and have all the proof that I am—his stance would have meant nothing to those men who would have taken his head in a second.

How can I be so sure of him being disingenuous? Maybe I cannot be. But I have heard the same arguments for murder at a local tavern by people who simply want to be one of the boys. Who say, with a nod, "I'll bury that prick."

So to say there is no evil, by connection, is to say there is no sin. All of this is fine by me—but I could ask him, why not recognize those who you applaud as having and holding to that which you yourself so emphatically dismiss; that is, the question of evil?

Saying this does not in any way elicit my sympathy for the casual brutality brought on in Iraq by a moral coma in Congress. As U.S. policy stated, "We won't have to fight them here," and thousands of innocent people are slaughtered, with a warning to TV viewers that "some of the images you might see are objectionable."

This conversation did, however, give me pause to think of the word "racist" and how it applies now, at times figuratively and at times literally, to those with whom we disagree, in the way the word "demon" once did. We no longer believe it shows displeasure in calling someone a demon. So the word "racist" has become the optimum anti-statement.

We who despise *they* can use the words "racist" or "bigot" to apply it to certain groups over our group in order to prove an inordinate humanity and courage. It becomes at times as trifling as believing that those with less education have less humanity. Or funnily, those who are secularly progressive are human and those who believe in God are not.

Still, this castigation of who is or is not the bigot in our midst allows some to dictate what humanity should be and, what is worse, to dictate who is or is not culpable. But looking close enough over the last two centuries you will discover girls and boys for every nationality and race—every one— there was/is always enough blood to go around.

———

Once visiting a former friend, I mentioned Solzhenitsyn's brilliant anti-Stalinist novel, *The First Circle*. I was very excited about it at the time, and the novel remains one of the great reading experiences of my life, but it also holds a secondary fascination. It deals with the idea of not only Dante's first circle but with the even more dangerous inner circle described by Tolstoy and C. S. Lewis, which I have been personally at war against from adolescence on. It concerns the need some men and women have to belong, a need so strong they give up their integrity and liberty in order to belong. I was trying to explain to my atheistic friend that people might do this at church—which he himself always held to—but they do it everywhere, every day, and no one revealed this better than Solzhenitsyn.

"Oh, but he's a racist," the fellow said of Solzhenitsyn. I said nothing else. The word was at that time, and still is, a fashionable register of strong personal disapproval, against people we disapprove of. *Racist*—as if that solves everything. Just as the word "demon" solved everything for the Grand Inquisitor. If someone is a racist, nothing else matters. In fact, you could burn bigots at the stake without a whisper of protest from those agnostics who have invested their lives in protesting inequality. Except I do not, nor did I believe the contention. That is I do not believe why the term "racist" was applied in this case. But it does answer one sticking point. For my former friend, and many others, have never read a page of Solzhenitsyn.

The friend knew little about Solzhenitsyn, but he knew when to apply the word "racist." It was a strange and enlightening experience for me.

Still, in the house where I sat for a few moments that far-away day, Stalin was acceptable, or at least benign (and had good ideas), and the writer who single-handedly took on the Soviet system that dehumanized half the world was not. It was an easy transference of moral power.

As well, my friend did not suffer as much as a blemish in saying "racist." It was virtually painless. Still, his easy summation, in some strange way, blessed the suffering of millions.

But there is something else about the word "racist" used too loosely (and I say too loosely)—it is knowingly championing a falsehood, or an intentional misplaced moral outrage to implicate someone according to your notion of dishonour, for benefits of self-congratulatory pretence. That is the way ethics are almost always applied at dinner parties. This is what has replaced religion and faith in much of our secular society.

Of course I am not saying that there are no racists we have to guard against and at times physically fight. The real problem is where you meet them.

I know you see racists in the white supremacy diatribes against three-quarters of mankind. And in the pudgy hands of Bible-touting zealots who would still burn most of us at the stake. But that's where we expect to see them. Yet I have met bigots in the feminist movement as easily placed as I have in motorcycle gangs. I have sat with them in common rooms at university—so assured of their intellectual superiority that they were not only intolerant but self-congratulatory in their ignorance of others.

I have met men in motorcycle clubs who believe nothing they do amounts to sin. I have met feminists who say sin is a patriarchal fallacy, to subjugate women. And I have met men at university who are frightened to disagree with these women—frightened of being labelled intolerant, and so permit such delusional intolerance.

But there is a trick in all of this, a sleight of hand. Both groups believe that being liberated frees them from the responsibility of sin and allows them to dismiss it as non-existent. I am almost certain, knowing both groups, that they have confused two deeply dissimilar human conditions as being one and the same—the search for liberty and the acquisition of power. It is really the acquisition of power, not liberty, that they are trying to attain.

This confusion allows for the same delusion, whether with certain of my friends at university or those in a motorcycle gang. Liberty and power are acquired by vastly different routes, and a person can only seek one or the other.

But what does this have to do with seeking God?

Everything, I am sure. To become liberated through faith is to not say there is no sin, but to be able to lessen its tendencies over ourselves. To lessen the mimic that exploits and forces us to try and be like others. And, in my mind, the only way we become liberated of this is through faith.

Most of the hurt done to people on a daily basis is of a coercive kind, the kind Orwell deplored, because it is so sanctioned by a social fabric that believes violence is always overt. This again is at the crux of my ongoing debate with certain intellectuals. But Orwell discovered that coercive violence always leads to the more deplored overt violence, and that it is impossible for one to exist without the other. Also, that people did not see this, or went out of their way to falsify what they saw or did in order to protect both the idea of virtue and their relatively simple idea of what violence was. The coercive violence in applauding the hijackers on September 11 should be recognized for exactly what it is. The young bicycle messenger supported the hijackers by saying he wouldn't himself be violent. Yet he already was, by his coercive applauding of violence he believed he did not exhibit. My only intention here is to say that this was attempted to be hidden by himself, and that is what concerns me. For if you do not want to recognize something for what it is, or hide it from yourself, that in itself is the main hedge fund toward compliance. This coercive violence is a direct challenge to us in seeking any kind of peace of mind, and in the ability to recognize it for what it is.

This, in fact, was Dostoyevsky's concern with Tolstoy's *Anna Karenina*. When Tolstoy wanted us to rejoice in Levin's proclamation that he would never be a soldier, Tolstoy was giving in to the idea of violence being obvious and overt—and worse, was simplifying it by thinking a man who wasn't a soldier was less likely to do harm. This is a terribly naive misreading of the soul, and my main contention with the bicycle messenger.

"My God," Dostoyevsky wrote, "if they [speaking of Tolstoy primarily] are our teachers, what hope is there for us?"

The idea, which Tolstoy himself knew was false, implies a moral hierarchy based on profession. Like my naive father simply assumed goodness in priests, so when I saw a priest's cantankerousness and hypocrisy, I was not allowed to assume my perception correct. But if I was able to throw off this yoke by the time I was ten, I am sure some of us who were *secretly* gleeful about the attack on the World Trade Center, because we believed Canada a better and more noble society for not having as many soldiers, should be able to as well. The yoke blinds you very easily if you think that the country that protects you is somehow at fault because your country is unable to protect itself, but your philosophy benefits directly from the protection you now scorn, and that you are correct in teaching the sanctity of this assumption. Then Dostoyevsky was right about you as well, and his warning about the greater implications of this tyrannical sin of omission is as relevant today as ever. For as Dostoyevsky knows, you can downgrade this assumption to fit any category or human condition and still remain self-righteously assured that others are at fault. What I am dismayed about here is the glee certain people I spoke to had, yet tried to hide by saying it was something else they were trying to evoke by being secretly jubilant that men jumped from the towers—to even say it was a concern.

But this type of qualifying humanity by institutionalizing professions, or categorizing jobs, or nationalities, allows us not only to dismiss people who worked in areas many could not, but after a time to not even consider them human. It also, by disassociation, allows us a moral superiority we do not possess; and it is the kind of moral superiority, which by our own kind of qualifying, we pretend is a search for equality.

Back when I was a student there was a good deal of moral outrage over the policy in Vietnam.

Some professors went to the States protesting the Vietnam War, secretly hoping to have students bait young National Guards—a confrontation that would put the professors into a story in *Time* magazine.

Tolstoy would know this was fraudulent in a second, but Dostoyevsky was one of the few to continually demand it be observed for exactly what it was. The coercive attempt to manipulate violence while melding it to one's own image of passivism, in order to sanctify us as human beings, shows how far we have blended what is untrue to what is sought as being true. It is the diehard secular obsession with intellectual positivism that Dostoyevsky warred against throughout much of his career.

But it is never the activism itself that is wrong. It is the application of activism as an instrument of passivism to promote oneself that leaves me deploring the act and questioning the motive.

And all of this has a subtle attraction to those who seek to promote liberty and justice within the context of a post-Christian modernism, which at times relies upon the same compartmentalizing and self-seeking righteousness that fundamental lay preachers might. In fact, both come close to being cut from the same cloth. We remember how certain preachers blamed the attacks of 9/11 on America's evil sins, just as the bicycle messenger did, without calling it evil or sin.

Most important is that faith is first and foremost individual. Much of our discontent—and our setting out to set up political systems, and then relying upon systems to tell us what to believe—stems from a yearning for freedom, and we often follow this trail to freedom blindly. When I was in university, waterbeds and hash became the new anti-religious props for a kind of generic intellectualism, the road to supposed freethinking through rebellion.

Many of us left university with these sentiments, and followed this road for a long time. Most of this was benign, and over time, outgrown. And I know that. And all generations experience it in various ways. But for some, this became more dangerous and more addictive.

So after a time, among certain people I knew, this idea of liberty and licence melded until there was a pernicious idea that crime itself was rebellion and rebellion was freedom.

There was one attitude that was strikingly subtle but firmly entrenched and duplicitous among some I drank with. The attitude even among some kind men that I knew in my hometown (and my hometown is no different from anywhere else) was that if someone was murdered, it was not their doing, therefore not their fault and none of their business. This was true. But one should realize the way this ideal promoted itself compared to how it actually worked in reality.

It was, of course, because of our close proximity to those who did commit these crimes, as well as our having to deal with them on a personal basis, as I and others did.

So, on occasion, those who sat and drank with some who had committed crimes, or were suspected of committing them, sat with those who had committed crimes against their neighbours, or against people they knew. But the reasoning by some was: As long as I am not bothered by these people, then I have no say in the matter.

But, of course, freedom cannot coexist with what this actually was—fear. There is no liberty in fear, there is only

power. Once again, it was mistaking two completely
dissimilar abstract notions, liberty and power. It is only liberty
that frees you—and the only thing we can attempt to be
greatly free from in our lives is sin—for one reason. Sin limits freedom and demands power.

So power promotes fear promotes sin—which so many I
knew, and for many a day myself included, said was freedom. Liberty in many ways among some people I knew had
been reduced finally to murder—the one sin to which all sin
aspires. Much of this had to do with the drug trade and the
secrecy around it.

The murders that I knew about were in the main done
with treachery, malice, and through venal opportunity. But
that some people wanted to think there was something
grandiose, and even were the first to shake the murderer's
hand, shows us the depths of irrational ideology one is willing to assume as free.

There was a feeling of personal omission during some
crimes that led to murder, where some of the criminals were
looked upon as somehow heroic by certain people who
believed they were exhibiting the best traits of freedom.
"Live and let live."

But live and let live was not really what this was: It was
self-interest. So the only way to really see this for what it
was, was to seek an alternative to it—and that alternative
finally was faith. There had to be a solution, a turning away,
and it had to lead to real freedom. I had seen enough of the
bogus kind. The idea that faith is something far away and
unattainable is silly—rather, I believe it is a profound component of our very makeup. Every single person, man and

woman, boy and girl, has it at their fingertips because it rests within the very fabric of our being.

Faith does not stop crime, or sin, or wrongdoing, or evil, or whatever we want to tag it. I am not saying it does, but it does always and forever combat it. For most of us, it is an essential platform for our daily lives. It is the one thing God gives us that we cannot refuse.

If we did not have it, even the most cynical of us, even the most dangerous, would not exist.

When I was a young man, before I had even a thought of all these violent actions, I was on a committee that had some authority on who would be allowed to go to the Catholic Youth dances. It gave me a fine feeling to seem important, when I was fifteen, even though I did almost nothing, except open a door or two with a key on Saturday night. But there was also something else. Most of the girls on the committee were socially elevated—and if I can use that term, middle class, I felt they were somewhat snobbish (though very pleasant), and more popular than I was. And I felt attracted to one or two of them, but mostly I wanted them to like me. In many ways I was a forlorn youth, somewhat of an outcast, and was very self-conscious about my lame left side. So I had thought that if I could get them to like me, then others would too. I am sure we have all succumbed to this at one time or another, and if you have not, then good for you. But I knew the moment I succumbed that it wasn't true—that this idea of purity and fine manners, of these young pretty Catholic girls and boys, was

simply a product of forced manners and planned piety—
and even though I did not swear in front of them, I had my
doubts that what they or I was feeling was at all sincere.

One Saturday night, a man who was in the group—an
older man in his thirties who had once studied for the
priesthood, and who acted as a kind of chaperone, for he
had little or nothing else in his life—took an epileptic
seizure in front of the stage. No one helped him initially,
and then two of the boys that I knew, who were under sus-
picion for smoking and drinking, went to his aid. They had
to drag him across the floor and make sure he didn't swallow
his tongue.

The next day I was surprised to get a call from one of the
girls, asking me to join a "secret" meeting. There we dis-
cussed the fate of the man who had taken the seizure. Certainly he could not come back to the dances, with these
"difficulties." We must take a vote and then go to the
priest. It was all to be done in secret, no one was to know.
But all of us felt very powerful at that moment.

I was overcome with a sense of responsibility and betrayal. I knew the man well. I saw how these girls and boys
shunned any notion of helping him, pretending to want to
help him, and how the two boys they had little to do with
did. Now they sat in judgement of a man with an illness,
saying that because of this illness he was unacceptable. This
in itself was deplorable, but no one seemed to think so. The
assumption was that we were actually doing this for his
benefit. We did not want to allow him at the dances, not
because he would embarrass us, but because he would embarrass himself. But there was even a greater falsehood

here. We weren't even concerned with being embarrassed, we simply wanted to exercise a power over someone else.

I, too, dutifully went along with them to the priest, knowing I had always been an outcast among these committee members, and would be still unless I voted with them. I remember to this day thinking the priest would dismiss our concern as being overdramatic or selfish. But that was not the case. The priest assured us that we were doing what was right. He, too, had been brought up exactly as we had been, to kiss the hand of authority.

He never said, "What you do to the least of these, you do to me." Instead, he said what he believed we wanted him to say, and he said it with forced piety. Then we all said a prayer and he blessed us.

I never forgave myself, but I want to say this, over time I did forgive the priest. I look upon him now and see him as a confused, hopeful person, wanting approval. He was trying to act the way he thought he had to, rather than the way he should. Looking back, it was I who knew better. But then again, we all did.

The man was not allowed back to the dances to act as our chaperone, and I quit the committee a week later. A year later I was put out of the dances at Catholic Youth at high school, and at the rink. All of it, to me, became posture and stupidity.

"Well, you are a real disappointment," the committee girl I liked said to me.

"Yeah, and you're an idiot," I replied. I suppose we both were right.

Part 2

The night I was born was two months before I was supposed to be. However, that day, October 17, is a significant one in my family. It was the day my grandfather died in 1924 and the day my grandmother died in 1965, the day my great-aunt died in 1969 and the day my uncle died in 2005, the day my sister-in-law died in 1999. It's not so strange then that this would make me believe in omens and such. Wouldn't anyone? I suppose there are those who would think of it as coincidence, and I would be the first to say they might be right.

I remember other things. The man who tried to get into the car downtown to steal money when I was alone in the back seat. The woman who refused to let my mother cross the street with groceries on a miserable day, when she had me by the hand. The time I promised my mother I could deliver a pot across the street and come back without being run over. Well, on the way back I was run over by a car. I went right under it, between the wheels, and popped out without a scratch. From that moment on, Kim, our collie, wouldn't let me cross a street alone. Even when I was seven or eight, he would hobble out to grab my lame arm and help me across. All of this left an impression on me. I was different from other people, and I must not be. But there would be no way I could conceal this difference, for it was a part of my very physicality, and I was at its mercy. For the most part, it was benign and for the greater part I was never bothered! Yet there is a vicious element in our nature that loves to mock those who are not the same, those who are out of step with the others. At times when I was mocked, I would look around to see who did not join in and silently applaud them.

One day, when I was about six or seven, a person who I thought was my close friend joined in when a few others started to torment me. He was afraid not to. In my own defence, I will say I handled all of this as well as I could. I am sure as well as most. I never in my life ran from anyone tormenting me about my affliction, and I could fight when I had to. That does not make me brave, it simply makes me stubborn. But I did hobble when I walked and had no use of my left arm for years. An open target, it made me aware of the mob. And it made me realize that it is the mob that lessens its individual sin by joining others to commit a graver sin that then could be lessened and even sanctioned—I learned this very early. By the time I was six or seven it was my strategy not to be near the mob. And when I was thirty-eight, and a person, who decided erroneously that I was brave, asked me if I was frightened of anything, I said: "The mob."

So then I want to speak about something that is peculiar.
I believe people do not think that mob violence is something
we see that much any more. It belongs to bygone tales of the
Old West or pioneer life, or at least mob violence is something we would not partake in ourselves. But what I have
been saying up until now is that the mob is the main stabi-
lizer of sin (or wrongdoing, if you will)—its main supporting
beam. The mob that turned against me now and again when
I was little is the same that turned against me when I was
twenty-four for writing things that they feared. Both believed that they were acting in accordance with honour
against that which they repudiated. But the mob fears much
more than they pretend. As Seneca said about Emperor
Nero, "One cannot give fear in measure one does not one's
self possess." That is, everything is measured out, and every
molecule of thought and action is in accordance with a
greater law. To do a shameful action can never be brave, no
matter how much the mob insists that it is, and sanctions it.
And the mob can be as active in the police department as in
the street. The mentality of people banning together almost
always follows the same logic and pattern in the end. René
Girard tells us that the idea to mimic in order to be the same,
in order to set up the scapegoat to be ostracized, is the way
not of faith but of religious zealots. Religious fervour of this
kind acts in accordance with that other condition—power.
The mob becomes religious fervour, no matter what kind.
So the mob is there to allow you to hide while still being part
of the action. The mob is there to entice one to sin.

Am I saying I am so sensitive that I can't take a teasing?
Hell, I was teased half my life for not being able to do what

others did, yet I insisted on trying. No, what I am saying is that the mob recruits the man or woman in order for them to sin, and therefore must congratulate them on doing so. It is not the sin that is the primary goal of any mob, but the congratulation that comes when one lessens their own personality to the will of the mob and is congratulated. The congratulation is never once said to be for doing ill, but for "being a regular guy" and "being one of the boys." That is what is applauded and actually that is what is sought. What they fear, more than anything else, is to be seen doing something that will not be licensed by the group they rely upon for comfort and support. Nothing lessens humanity more, and nothing in our society is more prevalent. Gossips are proof of this.

"Every sin is the result of a collaboration," Stephen Crane wrote.

And to say that this mob does not entice us daily in all environs is not to see clearly. I once said that I saw as much bootlicking malice in the common room of a university as I did on the streets of any town I was in. I was speaking about mob collectivism in thought and action, and how people mistook this for moral duty. The collective approval of a wrong action abrogates one's responsibility. I simply am saying that it is the same kind of moral duty that attends a lynching or an unfair university department "realignment." To gang up on a person and make them lose their chance at tenure out of fear of what others will say if we support them is the same as the man who stands back and says nothing when a man is hanged, or a priest and his flock who keep an epileptic away from dances and then bless each other for so doing (even if the lynching is the most ruthless).

There is a will among us to pervert these bullying events into just cause by the one thing all sin, even Stalin's, falls back on—self-righteousness. And self-righteousness is in the end the greatest curse man has.

The mob, just like the religious in the amphitheatre, needs the mob in order to be self-righteous, which is why self-righteousness is much graver an error than hypocrisy.

The self-righteousness of sin (or wrongdoing) is its main gloss, it is the veneer which soothes us if we wish to change the meaning or intent of what we have done in the eyes of others. It is far worse than hypocrisy, because it goes deeper into man's ambivalence toward truth. Or, in fact, supports our constant craving to change truth. This is what becomes of the Grand Inquisitor when faced with Christ in Dostoyevsky's *The Brothers Karamazov*—self-righteousness has changed the basic tenets of true to untrue, and therefore, in the name of Christ, Christ must die.

Hypocrisy knows the truth, and acts against it out of self-will, weakness, or desire. Self-righteousness bends the very idea of truth to accommodate a sin we can champion as being justified under the circumstance. There is no place in the world where self-righteousness cannot claim a victim.

In Milton's *Paradise Lost*, Satan is hypocritical in hell when he speaks to his right-hand man, Beelzebub. But what is a worse and more grave sin is the self-righteousness he gives to himself and his fallen angels, the duplicity with which he states his case, and the politics he brings to the matter. It is Milton's contention that politics was invented in hell through Satan's need to control those around him— to state a case for himself and have others agree with the assessment he has of himself. Politics is the one human endeavour that counts upon us knowing that a falsehood is being established as a truth, and relying upon the fact that the majority will have no qualms about this. That is, lying to please the mob involves the mob, in politics and everywhere else. The trait that Tolstoy expressed about the falsehoods of Prince Vasili in *War and Peace*—that the prince lived in a world where falsehood was so common no one cared that what they said was false. If we live long enough, we see that not only is this true but that many expect us to be false, and believe it is politically virtuous to be so. And this is how politics enters day-to-day life.

Again you might ask: What has this to do with a need to seek God? And again, the same answer: Everything. Our political nature is first and foremost an individual nature. Throughout much of our lives our own actual politics is often looked upon as benign and even justified, and therefore the duping of others because of being politic is somehow seen in many circles as being warranted (as long as it isn't overtly violent).

Everyone hates the politics that is utterly and shamelessly obvious, like the politics perhaps of Cheney and Bush, but no one minds the blush of insincerity when it comes from those we agree with, even if by its reasoning it will help ambush or destroy sincerity, and in the end destroy what may be truthful in an opponent's position.

I've witnessed it, just as you have in every political campaign and at every dinner party. It is still insincerity and it is still being insincere, but it is accommodated because we ourselves decide that the principles behind it are ones that benefit ourselves, or in some way benefit what we believe. This is exactly what Satan in *Paradise Lost* relies upon his friend Beelzebub to feel. Nor does it matter if I am speaking about the dual princes of darkness. It is exactly the same feeling that we share. And Satan uses flattery, deceit, and lies in order to do so. "Politics was born in hell," Milton says. But if that is so, then one should not blame the politicians.

There are those who will say that all of this is making a mountain out of a molehill, and therefore not worth mentioning. Yet there is not an evening-dinner gathering that goes by where these things are not seen for their cant and vacuousness. And if that is the case, something in our nature, some profound need in our makeup to counter these things, is telling us to do so. Not just to get it right, but for the feeling inside us that it is somehow dangerous to allow a wrong position to assume the value of being right. That is what is at stake here, and why these small things become important.

It is why Einstein's determination that "Christianity will never be explained away by a smart remark" is essential to our setting a wrongness right. The trivializing of so much that is fundamentally important is more than error, it can be a subliminal destructiveness that wishes the toadies of popular culture to be seen as heroic.

There are those who will also say that it is silly to use a bit of mythology written up in an epic poem to explain modern man. Well, that may be true, but man's inherent position is a bad one, for we always rely upon mythology to explain an unknown truth. And mythology follows us from cradle to grave. And from the Greeks to the Geeks. But within this, there are certain things we do know, and will know forever. Milton understood this as well as anyone who lived.

As René Girard says in his book, *I See Satan Fall Like Lightning*, Christians have gone a long way to try to de-mythologize their faith, to make it more palatable to today. Most of us dislike the idea of Satan as a physical entity, or what is more to the point, think that there is something slightly balmy with many who still talk of Satan as a real entity.

That is fine by me. So let us simply say, for argument's sake, that Satan is a *condition* we come up against. We all know in our hearts and minds this condition. We have all faced it at certain times in our lives. This nebulous condition is a profound one, and perhaps scarier as a condition than the actual entity might be if it does exist. And it is this condition that is resolved to destroy faith, and our political interaction with one another goes a long way to help this happen—to destroy faith in each other. Once that is accomplished, there is no telling where a lack of faith can lead us. Well, there is telling, though none of us would believe it about ourselves.

Politics starts in the individual. We are sometimes politic at keeping distances with those out of favour or fashion, sometimes politic with ingratiating ourselves to those who can help us or our family. And often we are politic if we disavow truth for our own benefit. If, for instance, a belief we hold is not shared by those we must impress, we disavow this belief in order to impress those who do not share it.

Then, if we are not very careful, the condition begins to

manipulate us to allow us to assume and take advantage—or gain advantage—by being dishonest with ourselves. Sooner or later we can take advantage only when we do wrong, because we have brought ourselves to a place that is wrong, and to travel back to the time of truth gets harder and harder to do.

All of this is political. We know it and know how people use it. It is how it was used in 1933 in Berlin, so that most of us, if we were there, would be politic at saying the things that would gain us favour, or at least not saying the things that would allow us to fall from favour. It would be only the very brave and principled who did not.

But what is this demythologized condition we won't call Satan? (I am not saying we have to.) Still, this condition creates for us everything that challenges our "better angels," if they exist or not. We know what bluster leads to, and deceit and insincerity. It comes at us from all sides, operating on all levels. We have come to expect it. And at some moments we feel enlivened by it if it is done to those we don't approve of. If it causes us to hate who others hate. As Simone de Beauvoir said, "Hatred is very often an exquisite feeling." The only problem with this is that hatred is usually a very poor judge of character. And sooner or later, hatred relies upon falsehood.

We know deep in our heart that there is something wrong in falsehood no matter how it is used. That is why, when the young woman in *Huckleberry Finn* chooses the poseur over her real uncle and walks over to hand him the money, it is a testament not only to Twain's understanding of human nature, but a comment on humanity's own wilful pride and need to be lauded and applauded for deceiving and being self-deceived.

We know this to be true from our reading of *Huckleberry Finn*, and not only because God has said: "God is not mocked; for whatever a man sows, that shall he also reap."

We know this is part of the condition—to allow ourselves to be seduced by a need for bogus trust (or faith) because we lack the courage to seek real faith. Bogus faith allows us to operate in the world, within the parameters of deceit and counter-deceit. To find that exquisite feeling of hatred again and again.

So by trading the word "condition," let it stand in for Satan. And when he blusters, we should not say he does not or would, or cannot, because he does not exist. We know that what is done, as condition, is untrue and self-glorifying, and this untruth is not only apparent but living, for we see it in others and in ourselves. So what is it? Where does it come from? The epitome of these acts has been seen, not only in this myth, brought to life by a great poem, but throughout the ages in every bit of treachery and malice recorded.

But there is something else that might suggest it as an entity—no matter how fantastic that may seem. For do we think about this condition as the *human condition*? Not really, for the human condition seems to me to be one which always pits itself against this horrible condition. This terrible "it," as Tolstoy calls it during the execution of innocent men in *War and Peace*. That is, these are two very separate conditions, and are not the same. In fact, the human condition's role, so to speak, is to seek an avenue where this condition cannot harm it. The very phrase "human condition" implies ongoing strife and war, and implies by its very nature this other condition—this terrible "it" that Tolstoy speaks about.

Still, we will all make up our own mind about him, real or unreal. But for some reason Satan turning into a toad and whispering in Eve's ear is far more real about the condition than the sum total of articles written in our modern day saying this myth is nonsense. Twain, who did not believe in Satan, nonetheless knew exactly when to put him in the room.

But this is a problem—hell. All religions speak of it, and all spiritual life is troubled by it—and our psyche does not let us relinquish it. As a part of the generic stamp of religion, it is present. It was used in ancient days to cow us, and it certainly still frightens us today. And it seems only faith can overcome our fear of it.

"I can swear there ain't no heaven but I pray there ain't no hell," the song goes.

"Out of nine lives, I've spent seven./How in the world do I get to Heaven?" goes another.

It is something that confronts our intellect. Even very great men think of it. "Of course God will forgive me; that's His job" Heinrich Heine said on his deathbed. And this certainly is what we wish for.

When Samuel Johnson—as brilliant and troubled a man as we might come to know—was dying, he called his minister to the bedside and said he was frightened of death because he was frightened of hell.

(There is a great moment in Johnson's life that came when, in an act of repentance, he stood with his head bowed on a street near his boyhood home because of some ancient disobedience against his father. He was jeered and scorned by the riff-raff passing by.)

"I do not believe there is hell," the minister said, reassuring him. And it wasn't just to reassure, but to instruct. But as men and women grow older many are less certain of the minister's comfort, and more share Johnson's concern.

The idea of dissolving or demythologizing Satan and hell becomes less comforting if we feel we are cheating ourselves. As we grow older, our idea of justice—that is a part of every human soul, that men and women of every age, denomination, believer and non-believer, hope and pray for—confronts us.

So most of us, at least once, come to ask: Where is hell?

Marlowe tells us, quite succinctly, in his play *Doctor Faustus*, where it is. We create our hell. It is above us and beneath us and about us on all sides. When we decide to be in hell, we are because it is in us. And the majority of us try to create it for others, if we are ruined by our own self-will. This is what the great movie *Citizen Kane* was actually about—the creating of one's own hell, and distributing it as far and wide as one can.

So there is nothing at all complex about it. As God does most things, He does them quite simply.

It seems to me that this is why seeking God is a continual buffer against those ideas that assail us as being virtuous without having virtue. Against the idea Satan has himself instilled in us that He simply does not exist, and therefore we need not buffer ourselves against sin because it does not exist as well. All these things that entice us have a beginning and an end.

Sometimes, in movies or plays, sin becomes divinity unleashed. It has, most certainly, in popular culture. Sin becomes our buffer against dogma. In comedy, this is always the suggestion—that sin is not sin if it is used against dogma. The trouble is that sin can slip the bounds of dogma pretty easily. Relying on the dogmatic assertion that everything is a sin, it coddles us sooner or later into mistaking vice for virtue and saying there is no sin.

I often think of the schoolboy, preppy bravado Mick Jagger attached to sin at his concert in Altamont. Dressed in his little devil suit—hoping to impress the Hells Angels themselves, while someone is knifed to death in front of him. What was he proving by it? He was proving that his rebellion could overcome the dogma he had suffered, and was immediately himself overcome by sin.

Sin is something we fight against, and at times bravely fight against. On some profound level, there is a sense that it is foreign to the best part of us. If this was not the case, it would not consume so many hours of our life trying to dissect it, overcome it, or, what is most often the case, find reasons to dismiss it as an illusion.

We know it exists because we commit sin and know when we do. We know it is outside the best part of ourselves by the way we shun it, and are mortified by the worst examples of it. We know we bravely fight against it because, once in its midst, it consumes so much of what we actually love. We know it is not an illusion when we are faced with its result.

David Hume said that there were very few things man could know, but one was the abstract, such as mathematics. In a strange way, I agree. The divergent symptoms that make up vice and virtue are abstract, and we come to know them well. And this abstraction that we know well is a parasite on or a blessing to our humanity.

Sin, as an abstract, can only be challenged by faith, which is also abstract and which many of us also know. In many ways this internal battle is the actual battle, the one ongoing battle the world over. All the other battles, economic and military, are a sideshow and are caused always by the internal, actual battle. When people rail at the religious thinkers for not doing enough, it is true as far as what is seen by us to be the problem; but many of them—many of the best of them—are confronting the real ongoing problems quite bravely, and it is not their fault that we do not listen or see.

Let us examine this, for a moment. Sin means transgression, and transgression means wrongdoing. So if there really is no sin, then there is no wrongdoing or offence—not really. So, then with no wrongdoing, no wrongness has been committed against us. Just a series of events that do not mean much to anyone. But most of us know this is completely untrue. That great and grave wrongs have been committed at times against some of us. And that what is so terrible about these crimes is that many times the perpetrator knows they were committed and does not ask for forgiveness because they are abstract and disguised. And we believe in our hearts he or she should ask for forgiveness. We also know we need justice because of these crimes. And we seek justice, too. Yet most of the time we never think of the justice we seek as really being man-made. There is, most often, some other form it takes. Sometimes we say, "If there is a God in heaven—he/she will pay."

Many times when we say "if there is a God in heaven he or she will pay," we are thinking not of a crime against ourselves but a crime against someone else that was/is horrendous, that as I said earlier made us shun sin and be mortified by it. That is, this is a universal declaration.

So we say this because we know that many of these wrongs, or transgressions, are not ones we can ever settle by taking someone to court. So often, the wrong has a sense of itself that is ethereal and timeless. Someday we think, in some way, we will witness justice. To those who have been seriously harmed, this is a constant wish, almost a palpable one. To the Jewish people and to the Palestinians as well. To the First Nations people all over the world. If we did not believe in this wish, and if we did not have faith in some greater good accommodating our desire for justice, sooner or later there would be no justice in the world. And worse, there would be no hope for or faith in justice outside our own physicality that would address the kind of transgression we know has happened. In fact, this is already the case. Very often there is no justice in the world, and the transgressors smile at us without shame.

So faith becomes not only an intangible anomaly but an actual principle. By this I mean that not only do we have faith, but in the real order of our psyche we need it as a part of our system of checks and balances, for our belief in a universal principle of right and wrong. And if this were a delusion, I guarantee we wouldn't have a belief in a universal principle of right and wrong. It would never have entered our noggin as something sublimely beyond ourselves.

When faith in the real virtue of unseen things deserts us, and we take matters into our own hands because we find it necessary to do so, then, sooner or later, we make justice unjust. For under our own hand, and our own particular brand of justice, what is just eventually becomes unjust, and everything—even civil law or religious law—may become unjust when we believe it is the principle upon which to settle scores. Every one of us has been hurt by this in some way.

So then, after awhile, unjust becomes what is natural, and when this becomes fact, faith becomes less and less important, and our belief in a final justice less true. This is what follows once we buffer ourselves against what we have done. This is the trickery we perform on ourselves to adjust what we have become to alter the circumstances. That is the spirit of betrayal and counter-betrayal wherein humans condemn humans through a hundred centuries, and it is abstract. As Hume says, abstract is one of the few real things man can know. What I am saying is that it is trickery to pretend that we do not know when we have hurt or done wrong, even when we are self-righteous about it, and everyone applauds us. Even if it is so subtle no one else in the world would know except the ones we have injured. Even if we are told or have come to believe that there is no evil or sin—we still know this.

To not take this seriously is in fact to not take anything in our lives seriously. But since most of us do take even the most trivial matters seriously, especially if they are things done against ourselves, then we should pay close attention to this as well.

But if this abstraction of sin is ignored the only thing that saves us is a refusal to believe in abstraction. For in the abstract both faith and sin rely upon the idea I have already stressed, "That someday if there is a God in heaven, these things will be answered." So to give this up is to rely only on ourselves, and to lose faith in the Divine. Especially if we are willing and able to turn right into wrong and vice versa, or convince ourselves that there is no wrong. We might remember the murders of the Bandidos Motorcycle Club last year. A settling of scores, it was even called a "cleansing."

The perpetrators of that crime were doing what is natural. What was perverted became natural. But if there is no sin, or wrongdoing, then to call this perverted or unnatural is simply semantics, just as the words "justice" and "betrayal" are, for so much of justice and betrayal— like the envelope of sin—is in the abstract.

But there is more proof of the human soul yielding to or countering sin. Because at certain moments such abstractions really take on a human face, and become visible to us. When someone says something terribly prurient or uncharitable, or malicious or deceitful, we suddenly see this abstraction as quite human. It bubbles up as a part of their physiognomy. It distorts the countenance. As those Bandidos being shot must have seen. So, too, do we see it when someone is delightfully honest and kind. Their features show a childlike wonder and happiness that embraces the entire world. And that I might add, the happiness in the soul to embrace the whole world, is the only way liberty can become power.

Perhaps there is a reason for this—that is, the physiognomy or look of good or evil is always something beyond ourselves, and we cannot hide it, though many of us try. And how do we try to hide deceit? Of course, by being urbane and politic. This in itself is a mask and guise that is intended to fool everyone, including ourselves. In the opening section of *War and Peace*, Prince Andrei knows very well how to wear this mask in society. It is akin to an expressionless, tutored veneer men and women wear in social settings where the discourse is untrue. When Prince Andrei attends one of Anna Scherer's soirées he wears this particular disguise. Only when he sees Pierre, his great, good, and childlike friend, does his expression change into one that shows his humanity. This is the private and public self that has much to do with the soul.

Wearing the mask tries to deceive who we are. It is that simple. For we realize that after a person says or does something, a startling form, a face has been revealed to us—and it either instructs us to evil or informs us to good. And not to see this is not to see mankind. But to see it is to recognize it as a warning or a blessing; that there is much more in the making of man then we normally admit.

How can we say we see this in each other, traits of good or bad, at moments that seem to delight God Himself? Who can be so sure that this is what we see? Well, first of all, it is evident to any of us on almost all occasions. But secondly, even if I am not sure, I believe there are those who can show us these remarkable conditions, and we know the conditions we are being shown and are moved by them forever.

Rembrandt being one. Michelangelo another. Van Gogh at his best.

"God is not mocked; for whatever a man sows, that shall he also reap" is not only a biblical warning, but a real promise in the faces of humanity that we have been shown throughout the ages. That we will reap what it is we sow. So the wrongdoing will be addressed in some profound and fundamental way, and those who have been injured from Africa to the Arctic Circle will in some way be redressed.

That's a good thing, to those at least trying to be good, which is the very vast majority.

And if it is a true warning and a true promise, it has to continue on beyond physical life, for nothing in physical life is certain to be redressed. Stalin shaking his fist at the abstraction above him is a warning not at what he shakes his fist at.

We might deny this, and there are times we might ridicule it, as I have as well and, if not careful, might again, but overall something in us refuses to stop the conversation with those abstractions. And most of what people ridicule, they secretly fear.

By being good, as I have explained, I do not mean being self-righteous on the one hand or pious on the other.

Goodness knows neither symptom, for both of these conditions are calculated. But true good is spontaneous. That is why so much that is actually good and healthy is deemed just the opposite by those in religious power. Yet it is the quality of spontaneous goodness that attracts us to children, and to men and women of courage. When the face wizens up and becomes deceitful we know that the person is calculating what he or she is about to say or calculating the response to what has been said. Nor am I saying that we are good all the time, or that we have to be even close to being good all the time. But there are basic tenets we believe in that will help us be good at the right time.

Let me tell you what a friend once told me: "A man injured me. I said to myself, if I see him again, I will simply punch him. That was that. I knew I was able to, and felt I had a right to. But as soon as I saw him, I was compelled to shake his hand—I felt vast warmth for him at that moment. I don't know why."

Well, I might answer, you calculated the punch—but you could not calculate your spontaneous reaction—and that was to be kind in spite of what he did or said against you.

Is all this fuzzy and warm and goody-two-shoes? No, puke that out of my mouth. This ongoing battle is as hard as granite as harsh as a winter storm. But that more people are like that man, and less like the one who would strike out is a good thing for us all.

I remember a line from an old movie by Val Luten (one of the unheralded great directors), where the hip artist who practises Satan worship asks: "How can you say evil is not superior to good?" Of course it is the wrong question, isn't it?

The question should be: Is evil better than good? On this earth evil has the superior hand. The aces and eights. It always has had. It infests every institution that pretends to be good. So evil does seem superior, yet is it better? Generally, the best of anything is never evil—or, to change the term, wrong-doing. So evil to us, even if we act evil, is anathema to "better." None of us would say a wrong act is better—or very few of us would say so.

But here is another problem that makes everything complicated for us. Bad is lots of fun. It almost always seems to be more fun than being good. And anyone who has acted bad—as I surely have, knows this.

"When I'm good I'm very good, but when I'm bad I'm better" Mae West says. There is more than a little truth to that. So why be good if being bad is so much fun? Isn't the very idea piety itself? That is what is told to us. Good is goody-two-shoes?

But I don't think that is true, because I do not consider the pious, the mealy-mouthed, to be particularly good. And to tell the truth, I do not consider Mae West particularly bad. There was less vice and more virtue in her truancy.

I remember the anecdote relayed to Samuel Johnson, about the acquaintance who said there was no difference between virtue and vice. To which Johnson replied, "Then when he leaves the house we better count our spoons." So why be good?

Because it has a lot to do with what Johnson said.

The need to be good is a condition that others rely upon. Humanity relies upon the fact that, in spite of the superiority of evil, goodness will abound, not because it is calculated but because, like that man who shook his tormentor's hand in warmth, it is a spontaneous reaction, in spite of the superiority of evil. That is the real portent of every novel and poem and play I have ever read. The truth being that without goodness, man himself would not exist. So then it is not simply a condition of some lives, it is a precondition of ours. But many of us are hell-bent on proving goodness wrong. But we should hope we never do.

But there is something else about this bad/good equation. It is the true secret of "being bad is better."

In fact, I think it puts it to rest.

Because, though we are somehow ashamed and feel betrayed when good people are bad, we like, even love, bad people when they are good. All of a sudden, they attract us like no one else. They become sudden prodigal sons. They rest in our own consciousness as our brothers and ourselves. In fact, they are what the bible suggests they are as prodigal sons. And this is what really attracts us to bad; we are attracted to bad when for some reason it suddenly acts good.

When someone who has a feared reputation is seen to take the side of the weak, we are suddenly enamoured. Because he shows a human characteristic that we need and want—and also in many cases shows this in a way which is surprisingly self-sacrificing.

"God hates a coward," the saying goes. And it is a truism that goodness cannot be cowardly, while deceit and treachery and malice—those things superior in this life—almost always are.

Mae West herself had this quality—that is, goodness, to show the virtue of kindness through the heady hair and painted cheeks. We never really believe she is bad, more than we believe she is kind. She becomes because of this, adorable, her weakness for sex a weakness we forgive because of something greater than her human frailty. That is her generosity and kindness to those around her.

That is what attracts the majority of us to bad. It is not the bad but the good that often shines through. It is what Graham Greene and Tolstoy knew about man. The delight in this goodness underneath. Nor am I characterizing sex as bad—it is the very last thing I would do. But the destruction that sex holds over us is understood, even by Mae West herself.

Still, the delight in this hidden goodness, which Faith ultimately relies on, is what the con knows also—and can exploit, without him even knowing he is exploiting it.

"I thought you were a good guy," the young boy says in *The River Wild* to Kevin Bacon's character.

"I am a good guy—just a different kind of good guy," Bacon's character responds.

That is, like Al Capone who fed the soup kitchens in 1932, he knew how to attract the susceptible to the con of being good underneath. But the great novelist Graham Greene knew this about the con, and knew how to separate it, to make us see the real value. So did Shakespeare, with characters like Tybalt in *Romeo and Juliet*, and so did Tolstoy in *War and Peace*.

No other character trumpets this essential paradox more than Dolohov, the rogue and duelist in Tolstoy's great epic novel, but ultimately we are disappointed in him, because for all his attraction the goodness underneath is a façade, and we become as painfully aware of this as does his young friend Rostov. That is, toward the end, he is outmanoeuvred by his own brutality, and his soul is gone cold, and Natasha is the one who sees it when she first meets him. Dolohov simply disappears in the novel, and after the war nothing more is said about him, because nothing more has to be said. He has had a thousand lovers, but he has never had love. While Pierre, the man he cuckolds, is the man who because of kindness and love finds truth and happiness. But what is strangely significant here is the truth and happiness were always Pierre's in ways they could never be Dolohov's, though the world clamoured to know and understand him, and give him respect.

There is a great scene about this bad/good equation, which I saw when I was a teenager and have never forgotten. It is in the movie *The Good, the Bad and the Ugly* and involves the desperado Tuco, and his brother, a priest, who Tuco, played by Eli Wallach, and Blondie, played by Clint Eastwood, visit for shelter, when Blondie is injured.

In a sudden moment, clandestinely witnessed by Blondie, Tuco is reprimanded by his brother, the holy man, for being a thief and miscreant, telling him he does not want him there, and that their father has just died.

Tuco listens for a moment, and then, losing his temper when his brother slaps him, slaps his brothers face harder and reminds him that it was he, Tuco, who robbed so that the family would not starve, and therefore allowed the priest to leave and become the priest he is. Of course it is pure melodrama, but there is also a wonderful moment and meaning to it.

Tuco back in the wagon with Blondie (they are on their way to harvest stolen gold from a dead man's grave) tells him that his brother begged them to stay, and was lamenting the fact that Tuco would not stay longer.

"No matter, even a tramp like me will always be able to get a bowl of soup," Tuco says.

That is, not only for his own, but his brother's sake, he lies again. You see, there is something unmistakably flawed about a priest dismissing a sinner. This is what Tuco understands and is shamed by, and he lies to protect his brother and hide his flaw.

Blondie, in charity, does not let on he knows the truth, and he hands Tuco a cigar, "After dinner there is nothing better then a good cigar."

We somehow suspect that Tuco knows that Blondie knows what has happened. Yet unknown to Tuco, since he left the room after he had slapped his brother to the ground, his brother had whispered, "Forgive me."

Pure melodrama, of course. Corny, probably. But as true as most discussions of right and wrong, and the social oxymoron that attends it. That is, the idea of sanctimoniously dismissing a sinner out of family pride, or most other things, was not Christ's instruction to the priests. It was, however, his warning to the Pharisees. What is also understood is that Tuco, from the time of his First Communion, understood this. What is open for debate is if Tuco was using his brother—most probably. But there was also a genuine love and celebration that his brother had become something Tuco was honoured by. And this in a way was a betrayal of that honour and celebration. This is not just a warning to priests—but to all of us. To the smug who turn on us. But there is something else, although it does not make Christ's instruction wrong.

Christ's instruction to us is what his instruction was to Saint Peter: "Upon this rock I will build my church." It is not the rock of the Vatican or of any other church, but the human foundation of knowing in our own heart what is good and valuable in the spirit. What is wrongdoing and what is not. The insidious flaw of the brother parallels, if not surpasses, that of his brother Tuco. This is what Christ warns us against.

Tuco believed his brother heard that instruction as a child and could see this. He was enraged to realize that his brother was still blind, that something in the church had made him so, allowing him that piety. In that moment the spirit of life was not in the priest but in the outlaw. Asking forgiveness to a departing Tuco shows us the priest suddenly realized this.

Chekhov wrote a story where we meet characters similar to Tuco and his brother, but with different results. The story involves a little priest collecting alms for the poor along the country road. Soon he runs into a man who positions himself as the priest's helper and confidant, insinuating himself into the holy man's affairs, and then he steals the alms. The little priest is left with nothing. In the last scene the thief is in the tavern and when self-righteously displeased by someone he shouts: "You watch yourself or I will get the police!"

This all has to do with knowing in our heart what is good. No one else can pervert good for us. To sanctimoniously claim that the church is nothing because it has perverted, etc, as some of my friends do, is to place blame on others that is impossible. That is, the perverting of our own intrinsic idea of good. Both the priest, in *The Good, the Bad and the Ugly*, and the thief in Chekhov's story have self-righteously perverted what was intended. They are, in fact, closer in spirit at that moment than either would admit. And both have buttressed themselves by a con. The con in the Chekhov story is even appealing, in a distorted way. The little priest is such a mark that it is only right for someone with the qualifications of the thief to take him for all he is worth.

But what Chekhov relies upon here is the last line—the threat that the thief himself will get the police—shows us exactly his comic smallness, and allows us to reflect on the little priest's courageous journey with compassion, and brings us much closer to our own hope for a courageous journey.

There is a courageous journey as well in the movie *High Noon*, with Gary Cooper as sheriff who just married that very day, Amy—Grace Kelly—a Quaker woman opposed to violence. These, of course, are old morality plays—but they are plays that must be observed. The sheriff has put a man away, kept the town safe from a man who is now out and, along with his brother and two cronies, are coming to exact revenge. (These people, like the mob I referenced, never act alone.) No one stands up for Cooper or with him. The town turns coward—and some profess their indifference—by hiding and drinking in the tavern, or profess their moral superiority by going to church and praying. (This tavern and the church are shown here to be one and the same.) It is interesting how all of these townspeople now turn on the sheriff and blame him, not only for his own difficulty but for the position he has put them in. The tavern and the church become the twin pillars of a false morality in the witnessing of one man's agony.

Cooper has to fight the four men alone, and he does— with Amy finally coming to his aid and saving his life.

Nothing shows better the idea of a pretension toward goodness enabling evil. For the surface good, the surface morality is neither.

Therefore what counts must finally be recognized, and it will be sooner or later. Maybe not within the confines of a two-hour movie, or a ten-page story, but someday and for all time. It will also be known what is actual violence and what is not. Those in church were far more violent than Gary Cooper's character that day.

In fact, I think I am saying what Christ and Tolstoy said: "The kingdom of God is within you." This does not mean I am against Mass or churches or mosques, et cetera. I go to church weekly.

Writers, of course, have taken on my church for years. Most, but not all (Orwell is a prime exception), are lapsed Catholics. Most, but not all, are writers I tend to admire. Some in recent years have pandered to the anti-Catholic bias within the modern secular audience—who expect to be told the things they are told—so as to enhance their reputations, and they have done so without a qualm, believing they are not being seen for who they are. Others have longer established reputations, and have been more heroic then their modern imitators, who have mocked without having to suffer. James Joyce is one who was heroic.

The Irish writer Edna O'Brien compares Joyce and Chekhov, and speaks about how they might act with one another if they met in heaven. She is right, of course—Joyce was a very great short-story writer and at points he did rival Chekhov. But it is his short stories that have the greatest truth. I like *Dubliners* better than his novels, which I have read with the exception of *Finnegans Wake*—which as much as I can tell seems to be a reconstruction of the creation myth in reverse. But I will say I admire Joyce very much, and I do not mind that he is an atheist—or that he says he is. Edna O'Brien, herself a tremendous writer, does make note of this, reprimanding herself beforehand, as to what James Joyce would say about her daring to propose heaven as a meeting place for our stellar literary gods. But I think her mention of this is disingenuous, as if we must all nod our heads penitently, realizing that a great man, suffering under Catholicism, would have no time for religion. (So many of my anti-Catholic former Catholics demonstrate the same conformed piety in their denouncements—and I guess it is their piety that I hate.)

Joyce's work is very religious, and atheism seems to be something that he never mastered. Or at least hard-core atheism is something he himself isn't at all comfortable with. It seems to be an afterthought of his cantankerousness, a bogus feeling that he applied to work that is great in the first place. To me, perhaps because I admire him so much, it appears like a trick he has played on himself, similar to what I did when I was sixteen. I could be wrong. I know many of his supporters and Joyce himself would say that I am. But if he was an atheist his work has God in it and he cannot escape this. And it seems in a way that when he comes closest to escaping this quality is when he allows his characters to be uncharitably in search of an alternative to God.

I will briefly summarize some of his disagreements with Christ and my disagreement with him. "Christ is a black-guard," a friend tells Stephen Dedalus, because he treated women—his mother, Mary—poorly. So we don't need now to believe Christ or the Gospels. Still, by reading the Gospels, do we believe Christ treated his mother poorly? And do we believe Joyce, even though we know he treated Nora Barnacle, his wife, poorly?

If we say Christ treated women poorly, do we overcome the fact that he allowed women to be with him and comforted widows and prostitutes who were scorned and levelled in a society that did, in fact, treat them poorly? That stoned them to death on the least provocation, which he stood up against? In many ways, was this the same society that existed in Dublin while Joyce was writing and in some ways treating Nora Barnacle poorly—perhaps on occasion like a blackguard?

My concern then is that this is posture. Joyce is not taking on Christ, he is taking on the nose-picking seminarians. He transfers his dislike from them to Christ, dismisses the Sermon on the Mount and the Gospels, but still gleans from the Gospels the nugget that Christ is a blackguard.

When he does this, Joyce becomes less appealing. The reason for this is twofold. One, Joyce has to step back from his story to investigate his reasons for the story—which is what he does with Stephen Dedalus in the last quarter of *A Portrait of the Artist as a Young Man*. And secondly, there is not one instance in his text that he really needed to do so to get his message across of reticence against priestly wisdom. (In fact, it was already done to great effect before he introduced the miffed intellectual willing to call Christ a blackguard.)

Still, if the forging out of the smithy of his own soul leads Stephen to the brilliant solution to refuse his dying mother's request to say a Hail Mary with her, or that Christ was a blackguard, then he has simply lost the beneficence with which he (and she) endured the world through three-quarters of his upbringing, in order to prove rebellion to Something that he says does not exist. Because the very Gospels he hates is still the text he relies upon through the wilderness of centuries to decide; well to decide in so many ways who is and who is not a blackguard. That is: "Let he who is without sin, cast the first stone" is what Joyce himself would want to say.

In *Dubliners*, "Counterparts" the innocent little boy pleads to his drunken father at the end of the story, saying: "Don't beat me, Pa, and I will say a Hail Mary for you—don't beat me and I will say a Hail Mary." Of course the boy is whipped.

The idea of not saying Hail Mary for a mother who all her life was a victim, and might be comforted to have her son say it, is the exact counterpart. Stephen has not grown or expanded from the role of the child, but has narrowed to become the father. Even if he is a far better man in the end, then that father.

In a way, through all of Dedalus's travels, and the terrible Catholic bigotry within which he grew up, the idea of the Hail Mary itself remains translucent and defining. I grew up with the Hail Mary, too, and blasphemed it when drunk, and realized finally what I was blaspheming.

I began by returning to those who knew the difference between style and substance. Once knowing the difference between style and substance was the testament to Joyce's genius. Then, somewhere along the line, he decided there was no difference between the snotty self-righteous priest and the Gospel of Saint John.

So what Stephen Dedalus must do is convince me that the Hail Mary is disingenuous, or that Christ, who is a black-guard, is disingenuous, or Ave Maria, as sung by the Cran-berries or Pavarotti, is disingenuous in order for him not to be.

Some might say he is denying Ave Maria for a different reason than Pavarotti singing it—but I will say the dying mother, or others, in attendance, who love her, will not take time to make that distinction.

This is neither a trite nor sanctimonious challenge. In fact, it is an essential one.

No one has to fully believe in the Hail Mary to say it with compassion for the dying. But in secret this is what happens. Most who say the Hail Mary cannot help for a brief moment but believe in its tremendous power to comfort. Try saying it without realizing IT's universal power.

That is my argument with *A Portrait of the Artist as a Young Man*—it mightn't be much, and I might lose, but it is still an argument. I do not deny Joyce's greatness, but in wanting us to believe Stephen's condemnation of a Hail Mary is greater than the simple kindness of saying it because he has somehow sanctified himself by dismissing Christ, Joyce negates the inherent search for kindness in the book. (For kindness is the only thing literature is seeking.)

Still, I would like to follow Stephen after he leaves his mother's side, and goes out of the novel, and walks away. Could there be a moment when he suddenly realizes he has betrayed, and the betrayal is not worth it? I do not know. He, of course, would say he has not betrayed himself, only those in the church who have betrayed. And I admit that the smithy of his soul forged a great novel. Joyce goes on, in *Ulysses*, to reveal his unending grasp of the genius of the moment. To reveal that, in our humanity, deceit and selfishness come with the parcel, yet can all be blown away. To quote the novel's young forlorn prostitutes on the street: "You boys from Trinity—all prick and no pence."

Part 3

I was looked at a lot when I was young. Poked and prodded. People wondered about me. Wondered if I would live, or how I would, and if I did, would I be the same as they were. That was the big crisis in their life, unknown by me for quite some time. How would I ever be like other people? Because for a long time—at least until I was five I simply assumed I was.

My parents especially wanted me to be as others were. My mother was desperate to include me in everything. But there is a wonderful indication that the oddballs in the end are the ones that sooner or later make the difference. It always did puzzle me how those who commend Saint Francis or Saint Joan of Arc still cringe at the fact that their own child might have a vision to do something out of the ordinary.

I did try everything. And it never bothered me very much at all. But my left side bothered certain other people, who then told others it bothered me. That is, they took their fear of my being different and placed it at my door. And I saw the fear of my being different in others quite early, because some people had it when dealing with me. Why did they fear me? Well, concerning my mother this came out of guilt for having fallen on the day I was born, and causing my calamity. It remained a block between us. She died in 1978 at the age I am now.

But knowing what day I was born, October 17, and what it means, as uncertain as that is to know, in our family history I am quite able to sometimes say that all of these matters were taken care of long before I was born and her fall might have had nothing to do with her. Being born, as I was, and in the condition I entered the world, has allowed me to see the world from a vantage point I cannot give up. Nor would I now even if they told me I would have played hockey as well as Bobby Orr (well, maybe).

For a physical body with two equal sides, able to do equal things, is as foreign to me as anything I can think of. It was not meant to be. That is all. Not now, or ever—except perhaps in a time I do not know of when in the afterworld I will be put together in the way the afterlife intends. That would certainly be looked upon as silly by most people. But I have no compunction to refute my own silliness. At least not yet.

The idea that how I came to be was predestined might make some skeptics think I believe myself to be quite important. But that is not at all what I am saying, or thinking. I believe that we all are predestined in ways we are not at all conscious of. Just as none of us know when we will arrive on this scrap of earth, none of us know really when we will disappear from it. My mother's guilt is understandable but not warranted, and I should have told her so many years ago—that there was absolutely nothing for me to forgive. But I did not think I had to until it was too late. Then I realized I was too late, and I couldn't tell her that it didn't matter. For I believe she always thought it did.

What my mother did give me was a love of the written word, and I suppose that was worth at least one fall down the stairs.

But seeing how I was looked upon as different has allowed me to see how people reacted to happiness and sorrow in their own lives. Many had a characteristic kindness I could never repay. But in certain respects, a few women saw me as someone they could needle and belittle for the failure of the men in their own life. And men, especially unthinking and cowardly men, tried to bully me from a very early age. It is true that some overcame the affliction of bullying as they grew older, but I still meet those who never have.

From early on, I knew that I was a special kind of target, yet it was never stated. Because to state it was to admit their own weakness, and fear.

What I did understand, however, and have ever since, is that both women and men sought the same level of cruelty if they did not watch themselves, and for the same ends if they did not know themselves and at some level this cruelty made me cruel as well.

There is a poem by Rick Trethewey which speaks to this: of the meanness in someone who is cruel to him becoming the meanness in him so he can be cruel.

———

My nephew tells me he must fight—because he will not back down. So at any time when he meets those who feel the same as he does, he fights. If they look at each other, they see in the other the hatred they themselves possess. And a fight breaks out, each blaming the other, neither seeing they are warring against the same kind of self. And most of these fights are not justified. But to tell my nephew this is to make him laugh harder, and so it is something he has to discover for himself. Still, what he must discover is something else again. Thinking this way will not make him fight fairly or choose opponents who can match him. He will revenge those who have picked upon him by picking on others who are weaker.

This is an ongoing symptom of enmity and friction across the neighbourhoods of the world, from East Los Angeles to the Rocks in Newcastle.

I will say now that I am no pacifist. When I speak of faith combating sin, I am not talking about having to pick up arms to defend oneself. There is a point to our warring that is sometimes essential to keep body and soul together. And I tend to (not always) look at peace demonstrations as having more to do with the ambition of those who demonstrate. As with the Weathermen, who were as destructive both morally and overtly to everything they oppose.

Even if we decided not to pick up arms and went far away from those who tormented us, they would be there when we arrived. For the world is constant and so is our difficulty in it. We, in our own nature, attract the same kinds of enmity throughout most of our lives. So the world plays out in a constant circle, and the state of war, not only between countries but between ourselves, is ongoing. This occurs privately and publicly, between citizens and countries.

Not any legislation can solve it. In fact, I do not think any institution or organization can solve conflict. I believe the only way to resolve all of what I have been speaking about is by relying on things that are not visible to combat, that which is in us, and which is tangible but invisible as well. If we rely upon these things that are not visible, we will pay a price of being called superstitious or silly, but it will bring us out of our dilemma—to a sound faith, with a realization that the world has more than one dimension.

Yet, how can we know that there are things that are not visible, that are "other?" We wake up to them every day. They are not visible but present. The idea that this is so, that there are other things present, is almost impossible to eradicate from our being. We try to deny it through other emotions. And almost all the emotions we use to deny these things are in a sense negative and life-defeating. For we are trying to deny that which we must deny, because in our heart we feel it does exist. And it bothers us that it does.

In fact, why deny something that is not there? If you point a finger at it, it makes what is not, what is! But what is so spectacularly self-deceiving is that we are spending time denying what we feel exists—and what we feel exists is the focus of our denial.

I believe there is not an atheist in the world who does not rely on those invisible things himself, though he or she might mock that which they rely upon and call them by other names—luck, chance, fortune, hope, whatever it is that makes us think that a life mapped out is not in our power. If we mentioned this to some, they will tell us that this is a product of hocus-pocus or irrationality, a naivety planted by generations of conditioning—and not something positive that rests within the very cortex of human experience.

It seems a sham that our true and real and one destiny is in the power of things we do not know or, more importantly, cannot see. But what do we know? How many things happen in one day that we are not conscious of, which will thrust us forward in our lives, that we say we are convinced is under our control?

A pregnant woman goes out to bring in the clothes hanging on the line and does not tie up her laces, since she will only be a second. Yet she trips and falls. Only a moment before, the child inside her was complete. A moment later its left side is damaged forever. So what? Well, I am not complaining, but I am assuming that something else was involved. And after a lifetime of thought, I believe my mother's fall had nothing really to do with her. It was not to her benefit or detriment that she fell, but to mine. (I am not making light of her remorse or concern.) Her hope for my future was delayed—thinking I would not live, and if alive, would not function—and then modified to contain the problem.

It was in the modification where I found hope of God. I don't kid myself, either. I rarely talk or look like I have hope in God, and have as many problems with people as you could name. My left side has made me the subject of derision, but it has not taken away the foundation that I have come to believe in.

I have not met an atheist or an agnostic who would not spurn this with intellect and yet does not have hope for the future themselves. And makes plans for a future they do not in the least control. But by planning and hoping, they do believe they control. And they speak of those plans to the silences about them, and beg those silences to understand. So their belief in hope is not so different in kind from mine, nor mine from a priest who prays to God. In fact, by extension, the atheist is not different in kind from a priest, but only in degree—something perhaps neither would agree with.

The priest implores God, the atheist tells us there is no God to implore and then somehow blames God for it. That is what I used to do—almost. I once blamed God for everything.

It is like the comic who said he disbelieved in God, but blamed Him for all his problems. He was an nag-nostic.

The modern atheist has done this by blaming our terror on religion, professing to us that getting rid of religion would be the final nail in God's coffin. And he is partially right. He is right to sever the connection between God and the terrible sins of modern religion for a reason he won't imply. It is that God exists independent of what the religion he rails against does or doesn't do. The atheist is like the reverend who takes money for his $10-million house; he seeks a relationship between God and religion that isn't there. What the atheist forgets is that severing the relationship between God and religion is already done by those who don't seek God while claiming a religion—but this is not really what the atheist is after. He wishes to sever the relationship between God and you, in the same way he believes he has done it between God and himself. Then he will be satisfied. But if this was done, what would happen? Well, it has been done. The schism was forced on a hundred million people, with godlike indifference to God. And, worse, an absolute indifference to man.

Once this happens, something else must follow. The atheist will look around and say, as did the fictional Napoleon, the pig in *Animal Farm*, "What next?"

And "what next" will always and forever be closer to what we've already witnessed. It will be closer to Vladimir Lenin's proclamation of assassination than to John Lennon's self-indulgent song "Imagine."

The actual Napoleon said, "Men of my stamp do not commit crimes."

I have seen many who are men of that "stamp." At least they believed themselves to be. So, in a way, they were no different than Napoleon. I have seen them and drank with them. They were the ones prepossessing enough to believe that the laws that regulated most people did not apply to them. That for some reasons the laws that applied to them were different. And they went a long way to show us that they were. Not all of them committed the most ambitious sin, the one other sins aspire to—the sin of murder—but many I knew actually did. And I knew some of the victims, and in their workday world some of them would have committed the absolute sin as well if it was not done to them.

Am I talking of self-defence here? No.

But let us look at the mitigations for this crime. There are mitigations for the act of murder, such as self-defence, etc., that most of the people who commit the act immediately fall back on to purify it. But one might ask, if it was actual mur-

143 — God Is.

der, why do so? Why do they wish to purify actual murder, to make it what it cannot be? For the reason they committed the deed was to prove in so many ways that the laws that applied to ordinary men did not apply to them. This is what many who committed murder held up to those people whom they knew. I knew them, and they held it up to me. Many said, "Do you know who I am?" As if we should know being who they were gave them this right.

Bear with me for a second.

If even the crime boss Meyer Lansky claimed he committed no murder, though he had others kill for him, what is he trying to imply? And what does it imply about the act itself?

I believe the act of murder, the champion of all sins, is a changeling—its own entity that seeks attention, on one hand, and tries always to distort or hide its own nature, on the other. It constantly needs to be onstage while at the same time not be discovered for what it is.

It is as if some of the men who have murdered have allowed themselves a longing for something abstract within themselves to blossom, and once achieved, they suddenly have to deny that they ever longed for it. Could one say that about rational thought? No. But rational thought has been replaced by rationale. And this rationale is a justification, even a faith in sin. (Or wrongdoing, if you prefer.)

In the act of murder, sin becomes faith. Certainly Napoleon saying that men of his stamp do not commit crime proves that he has put his faith in some other place— in himself being above the laws that govern the rest of mankind. So faith in sin taken to its logical conclusion becomes murder. Or the idea that he controls and decides what is and what is not sin. And this necessitates an internal discovery of oneself in some way, a kind of growing toward Something, which is not just physical. And it is not the physical aspect of murder that is ever its most telling aspect. So there is certainly another aspect—and this aspect relies upon a belief in the veracity of murder. It believes in Napoleon's statement—just as Stalin and Hitler, and many throughout history, believed in it.

The act of murder is, in a way, the sublime anti-miracle that wishes to appeal to people in a similar way that a miracle might. The taking of life is, in a way, the miracle of people who refuse to believe life is a miracle, or at least have registered their superiority to people who believe such foolish things.

But after a murder happens, many of the perpetrators realized they had conned themselves or were conned by the abstraction that Hume spoke about.

Some are ashamed, of themselves and of their crime, and immediately confess. Most are frightened to be called a murderer. And it is not just their fear of society's disapproval.

Many times the act is actually a horrible and cowardly one—there are all kinds of reasons for this sudden reversal, of trying to take back what one has done in so much false glory a few hours before. They run, they hide, they pretend it is not what it is, that the sin has not happened.

But my question is about the fact that belief in the premise arrived at before the murder—that "men of my stamp do not commit crimes"—is in some ways now noxious to them. Why try to lessen its value to yourself if you were the one who aspired to it for years, built up to do so, inspired fear and hatred, and managed to get it done? And after all that time, you have finally, from petty sin to murder, accomplished what something inside you set out to do.

Where you showed your physiognomy as not being good and childlike but, being malevolent and self-glorifying—and suddenly you want to take all of that back! Why in hell would you want to?

In the last few years of my drinking, I mainly lived in a world of murder, where the murders were perpetrated not by reason of self-defence but by other more venal motives. There were ten or twelve murders that happened about and around me within a period of two or three years. But there could have been many more, and some of the people I knew protected themselves by ascribing to murder, or at least they showed a disregard for its implications. I suppose they had to.

The idea was this: Judge not lest ye be judged.

That is a great statement, but like all statements of truth it must be used in truthful ways.

I knew from the time I was twenty that no harm would come to you if you got along with those who murdered—much, very much like the boys in the bar in the movie *High Noon* did. So one must be respectful to those of us willing to commit the greatest of sins, and if you are respectful, no harm will come to you—unless, of course, you are seen to be weak and vulnerable, and alone. And if that is the case then you too might come under the gun, and those who say, Judge not lest ye be judged just might not help you either.

In a way certain murderers (not all, but those who know

how to exercise the con of being good underneath) are held in reverence.

"Do you know who I am?" one of these boys said to me one night, as if he had become special since he was supposedly willing to kill.

But to get back to the question of why one, who had honed up for it for over a decade, finally, when a man is sitting across from him, takes out a shotgun and blows his head off, so the brains are on the table, and says, "Looks good on ya."

Then he gets his wife and children out of the house, and telephones his friends, who have jointly succumbed to the same idea—that the one large value in their life is the ability to take life because it causes fear and terror in others. Why then does he sit in a car and bawl, and say it was an accident—and they must prove it was an accident? That the gun shouldn't have fired?

Oh, jail, yes—there is that, of course.

But there is something else. Something this boy didn't quite expect or could not escape—it has to do with the actual sin. The sin of murder is in itself a damn coward, and shows its true nature when it is revealed as such. It is in some ways its own breathing entity. Its form changes like that of a chameleon, bloating up in front of Death as Satan did in *Paradise Lost*, to being that of a toad sitting on Eve's ear. Milton wrote this not because there is no passion to glorify death and sin, but because there is, and always will be. Up until it is experienced, there is a need and a craving to experience it within our society in a hundred thousand ways. But once it has been experienced, it becomes what it always was. And once again you are going to say I am exploiting a myth to make a point. And again I will say this myth is entirely relevant to the point—and would not have endured as a great poem if it did not have relevance.

That's the real reason for the change in attitude. The evil intent of the sin to glorify itself flees from you, from the internal you, and you are simply left with the sin, and the false glory. Napoleon's retreat from Moscow is, as Tolstoy tells us, just this—the flight of someone who must escape from what he has done. If Napoleon did not see this as his role in an internalized history—where the real battles take place—those many around him during those awful days did. They not only wanted to flee the war in which they had invested their souls, but they needed to be free of him and his falsehood.

For you have invested not in life and courage as you were made to believe, and falsely wanted to believe, but you have invested in death and cowardice, and now you reap the reward, and can, deep down, be nothing else. That is the abstract and hidden world we can believe in, for I have witnessed it in a dozen courtroom dramas, and in a dozen barroom brawls.

This particular sin of murder makes a proclamation that you are above other men in a kind of wanton bravery, similar to the "wanton troopers" of Marvell's poem "The Nymph complaining for the Death of her Fawn."

Then you finally realize what it has allowed you to do, instructed you to do, and then it has left you on your own to face the court and the people around you. This is what the act of murder states—your private self is a venal one exposed to the public.

So he might realize, after years of bravado, that what he has actually done is a sin of hubris a hundred times greater than the others he has committed. And the hubris is cowardly, because murder almost always is.

"You have done what you have done" the voice tells Alex in my novel *The Lost Highway*, when he tries valiantly to make excuses for himself.

So the complete reversal of Christian proclamation has happened. The killing of a defenceless man is thought of as brave, and Christ on the cross is thought of as spineless, until both events are over. And once they are over, the world reverses its axis. To be confronted by this again and again, and not to see it for what it is, along with its implications, is to concoct a misplaced sentiment for our own comfort.

Two novels, *Crime and Punishment* and *Oliver Twist*, present the most fascinating study of this, with Raskolnikov, who talked himself into murder, and also with Bill Sikes in Oliver Twist. Both are profound studies of the power of man's psyche building toward the ultimate sin, and how each person decides there is no sin yet commits it, even if the person remains relatively unaware of the terrible process involved. In Raskolnikov's case, the end is the beginning of his redemption, the beginning of faith. That does not sit so well with secular people—the end cannot be the beginning.

Yet there is something to think about. If these terrible processes were not so, why would there be so much ultimate truth in the telling of them? If these things were not so, why would the breath of faith, at the end of both novels, negate these terrible acts?

Bill Sikes, after bullying and torment and deceit and treachery, after he kills poor Nancy, must get away. And he runs to the rooftops, gets caught up in a rope and in ultimate

justice is hanged accidentally. Bill paid the ultimate price for
the hubris of sin.

Yet, when it does happen, a murderer often feels no more
in control of their destiny than the victim.

They suddenly realize they have been used—but how?
They have been used by something beyond them, perhaps
beyond their own time and space, that is, the self-perpet-
uation of an eternal clause in man's makeup. The secret of
this sin is its uncanny ability to transform vileness to glamour
and then, in a second, return us to our understanding of
how vile it all is.

Worse, it is the final submitting of what you believe you
have to Something else. The idea of self-will, propelling you
to this, is what you actually give up the moment you perpe-
trate what you believe your great self-will allows.

Many have said that they were in a trance or could see
themselves outside their own body, looking down at the
crime as if they were witnessing it on television. Many will
say it had nothing to do with them. In some strange way,
they may just be right—they may have been used by
Something through their own hubris to exact a penalty on
others, who, in many cases, are much like a mirror of
themselves—and it may be the exact same thing that used
Napoleon, or visited Stalin at the last moment.

It may be—it just may be exactly the same.

I want to discuss what has brought me to faith, or at least
to the realization of how immensely underrated faith once
was with me.

I think there are but two or three writers in Canada who have seen more of the world of violence than I have. Violence and the threat of violence existed near me for years. I am not saying my town was different than other towns. I am saying my town had what other towns had, and do have. Most of the people on my river are kind to a fault. Many of the criminals I know are as well. That is the truth. Yet there are those who are not. I knew a man who knifed a piglet on a dance floor with his Buck knife, and another who had a pit bull he would beat in front of people. When anyone tried to stop him, he would order the pit bull to attack. Then he would go back to beating it.

These things, horrible in themselves, showed a constant degradation of the spirit through the idea of power. And the one thing power does is limit freedom.

Also, men I knew murdered or were murdered. Men I knew raped and burned people out. The last meal one man had was a moose steak I took to a hunting camp. He was hungry and was fed, and killed a man later that night and then was killed himself.

I knew a boy since he was a child who raped a seventy-five-year-old woman and killed her husband. My father's house was burned by a man who had killed five people.

Many who were in close proximity to these people found ways to define themselves so others would not bother them. Convention allowed some to become more like those who perpetrated crimes so as not to have crimes perpetrated against them. In many ways, I am not criticizing this at all. How do you deal with crimes that are close to you? There is a part of the social fabric that is generally left alone, for their respectability and professions are in many respects a shield. So if they do not confront criminals head-on, to a great extent they will not be bothered by them (unless, or until, they are forced by some circumstance to defend themselves or others). Then there is a part of society that is not left alone. They have been born or grown up in close proximity to the criminals. This part of society, the second part, is the more vulnerable.

"I am too poor to be moral," Eliza Doolittle's father says in *Pygmalion*. And I understand his claim completely.

I drank mainly with many of those from the second group. And as I wrote in *Lives of Short Duration*, the idea of drink replaced the idea of the spirit by allowing the drinker to pretend it was one and the same.

Yet as many middle-class people turned against what I wrote, especially early in my career, I became a target of some derision in my own hometown. And certain people who existed on the derision of others realized this. And so I, too, became a target after awhile. I am blaming no one, it was simply that way.

I became aware that small crimes lead to bigger ones, not by socio-economic conditions, or daring, but by something more ingrained in the nature of man, some self-aggrandizement that seeks to lessen the humanity of others around him by doing so. That's not a new theory, but I am not trying to create one. So like Gulliver coming home from the land of the Lilliputians, screeching at others to get out of his way, we become puffed by delusion and by fear. This is what had happened around me and, in some ways, to me over the course of fifteen years.

So stumbling toward the sunlight, I, like a billion others, sought faith in the end. I, at the last of my drinking, was to arrive at my beginning.

The trouble is: where do we find this faith, where is the miracle, and when do we perceive it working in our world? I knew that even the church did not see it when it happened at times, and questioned it. Saint Bernadette and Saint Joan of Arc are great examples of the church's persecution of the holy. Were these two young girls holy? Absolutely, without question.

So it bothers me that they who now have statues to Saint Joan and Saint Bernadette are the same as the ones so infused with malevolence toward them. The church has in some way allowed itself to lose its idea of what faith it must have and what faith must be, or strive to become. It has played the game of compromise.

Faith is a door always opened—you can jump in or out at any moment. But if you jump out, when you go back in, you start all over.

In the world of faith, those who could not compromise got far enough away from the door and then found, in the end, that they had nothing else to rely on but faith.

That is the road of Saint Francis—and Saint Francis does not demand we follow him but begs us to realize he cannot compromise. No matter whether we believe or disbelieve, there is hardly a man better.

In some way this is why Pope John Paul II infuriated so many Catholics, especially those who thought the faith was supposed to change with the times to become more acceptable to what they considered virtue. They were waiting for

John Paul II to liberate them from the obligation of their faith. Now, like him or dislike him, he could no more do that than I could. The only one who can liberate you from your faith is you. And it is easy enough for you to do. But since he could not do so, many people I know, who are kind enough people, condemned him for it. But he himself had no choice in the matter. For what he was saying more than anything else is that faith will solve the worldly problems people are consumed by.

No matter how they criticized him, I believe he, more than any man of the age, was able to say simply: "God loves you," and more than any person on earth, be believed.

I have a recent copy of *Maclean's* magazine that says the church does not need Christ any more—that certain scholars believe the church (I use this in the generic term) would be better off without him hanging around. This is said as if it is new, and as if it is provocative. It is also said as a way of pretending to be taking the church's side. It is not at all startling to find a modern-day scholar who can tell us what Christ really said, and plead the case that Saint John or Saint Matthew cannot because Christ was dead when those prophets began to write.

I have met lapsed Catholics or Christians who argue this. And they are furious that a man who they sometimes think is intelligent dares to argue back. Or really not to argue. Because there really is no argument. No argument can increase or lessen a person's faith. That is why debates, in the end, are foolish. No one who believes has a hope of proving anything other than that they have faith. For faith has nothing what-soever to do with this. And it is my contention that the one thing people cannot deny is an abstract they must conjure to negate. The idea of Christ's non-existence becomes impos-sible because he is an ethereal transmutation of our own consciousness. That is, the transmutation takes place the moment we deny his existence, and we are forced to create him to do so. And Christ is aware of this, even if he is a man-ifestation of goodness, simplicity, and truth.

Why do some say the church does not need Christ? Because he is, after all, an embarrassment. His miracles are best if they had not happened, and our hope for the afterlife has to be tempered by all the valuable science we have learned (or believe we have learned).

That's the plain and simple of it, which, in the realm of true faith, has no meaning. But true faith has no dog in the fight—for it cannot explain itself and will not excuse itself.

"Peace which surpasses all understanding" is what faith actually is. It is nothing less than a complete transcending of earth, of geopolitical concerns. That does not make us comfortable, nor can we always achieve this. Yet it is a tran-scendence of murder and horror, not a participating in it. It is a transcendence of what is not living or life-affirming toward what is. That is all.

Why is any of this important? For a long time I won-dered why.

Faith is important simply because all of mankind's other concerns are actually unsolvable without faith—and great faith.

To say you are going to talk about these other concerns as a surrogate to faith is to miss the point of what Christ intended and only what faith can overcome. This is what I discovered drinking in bars with those who murdered when I was thirty. For many who murdered had all the desires and conceits that I had and were no worse than I was in many ways. In many ways, their idea of what was good and bad was shared by most people with whom they drank and cavorted. Therefore, if so many attributes are the same—in fact, there is hardly a murderer I have met whom you would not like in some way—what do we need? Well, if nothing really matters but ourselves, then we need nothing else. But if we see these tendencies as an internal war waged against ourselves as well as others, then we need faith to combat these conceits.

So where is the miracle and where is the faith?

Well, that is why I wrote this polemic. It is still forever and always all around us.

Where do we find God? Where do we look for Him?

The atheist will say that we cannot, that history has doomed our search. But then I have never really trusted an atheist to tell me the truth about what I should believe; for, by his very nature, he is in constant denial of the wonder found in himself, of the very transmutation of God inside himself.

This might be, because there is not one atheist I have yet met who has Tolstoy's three conditions for greatness: goodness, simplicity, and truth, more than those he always dismisses.

Because goodness, simplicity, and truth can be had and maintained—and maintained is the word—through one condition only, and that is faith. It is why Princess Maria is essential to *War and Peace*. It is also why faith is opened to children, and why virtue is always seen as childlike. These are the obvious conditions of faith that man tries all his life to replace.

Goodness, simplicity, and truth are what everyone seeks in others and wars against in themselves. It is an oxymoron of policy, and if we war against our own goodness, simplicity, and truth, we find ourselves battling the very foundations of faith. This is what Tolstoy was trying to tell us, when writing about such great figures as Napoleon. The pandering to greatness, the whimsy, and the self-serving insincerity of Bonaparte are all looked upon as greatness unbounded, and are dissected by Tolstoy to be seen as vacant and empty. Most of Bonaparte's statements are really a symptom and a condition of this emptiness, and simply show the world.

"A man of my stamp doesn't commit crimes." It is not the word "crimes" that bothers us, but the word "stamp."

Of course we all say this is what we desire—goodness, simplicity, and truth, and at times every day we maintain it. But it is certain that we fail. We all do. But some of us, many of us—at times most of us—blame goodness, simplicity, and truth for our failure and begin to mock these three signposts, even to the point of being revolted at anyone who possesses them. Then we become skeptics of the very faith that can re-establish these conditions and bring us to an understanding of God.

God is. In fact though we rarely, if ever, acknowledge this, how in the world could *He* not be. To not have God present would stop forever the dialogue that is carried on, in all moments and at all times, with the universe unbounded around us. In fact, what is the world of art and letters crying out for? How many books and poems and paintings and how much music, in conflict with God, is really arguing with Him in the very same way Job himself did? And what we see, many times, through the beauty of these paintings and books is not the absence of God, but the presence of God in the argument, which makes the art so necessary. In the very agony of our argument, He answers us through the paintings and books wherein we try at times, and exert all our energy, to refute Him. And He simply says, "Be still and know that I am God."

"This too shall pass."

That does not make faith any easier. And to know our own day-to-day problems makes it harder to realize that "this too shall pass." Not only this, but the very fact that you must recite "this too shall pass" means, of course, that something you do not want in your life has happened, and on occasion, it is not just something, but something horrendous—a betrayal by a spouse or friend, the death of a child, a reversal of fortune so great that you cry out like Job. And so your faith is in agony and is lost. You become like CBC commentator Gordon Sinclair, railing against God for demanding faith to believe in Him, after he lost his child.

But this is when faith begins. As one theologian has said: "Faith begins where to the unbeliever proof in the absence of God is substantiated." That is, faith begins at the cross. I do not know why that is, but I have seen it all my life. When Christ says, "Pick up your cross and follow me," he is not saying look around and find one, suitable to the journey. He is saying you will have one given to you that is most unsuitable and you will hate to carry it, but you will have to. The fact is, whether or not you believe in him, the cross will still be there. You will, in so many ways, still carry one. That is the secret.

Nero beheads Saint Paul for not calling him God, and then has his bodyguard slice his own throat when he himself is condemned. In his last moments, he rushes from place to place, trying to find a friend to hide him. He wants to drown himself and finds the Tiber too cold. He then crawls into the basement of an empty summer villa, and laments that the world will be empty without his great singing voice. Then, unable to plunge the dagger, he has his bodyguard do so.

This is not simply literary justice, but a profound statement on the nature of universal ideology that goes beyond the common law or Napoleonic codes of justice, into a far greater impartiality we are not personally in command of— and can never be.

Not once in our lives do we have the ability to foretell what will happen to us. If that is the case, as I know it was with me my entire life, why do we think or hope for justice and fair-mindedness, and why do we exalt when this happens even though we have no control in determining the outcome? Why do most of us, when we are unjust, pause and examine ourselves and hope to do better? What would it matter if the meaning of Nero's and Saint Paul's death were the same? And I guarantee this: if they were the same, we would have no reason to compare them now.

Which brings me to another point—the idea of miracle and justice and wanting the world to make things right. If we use Nero's fate as a simple mechanism of universal truth (nor am I gloating at his fate)—then in the end, the truth will not change. And as horrible, as truly horrible as human inhumanity can be, "Be still and know that I am God" is not only something we have to rely on, but something we can be assured of. Some will say this is religious theatrics, and yet nothing they ever do themselves will improve the case of humanity, or truly lessen suffering, even their own. So it is a theory that goes far beyond their disgust with the proposition. And this is what they sooner or later will have to face.

The choice is between faith or nothing. And if sin exists with faith present, look at what happened when Stalin created nothing. You might say one accomplishes only what the other does. Many of those believing in Stalin thought so too, until Stalin decided not to believe in them.

So, like many of these men and women, most of us do not think of these things at all, until we are ourselves faced with a dilemma the nature of which is on many levels twofold—personal abandonment and private degradation, of one form or another, by a world we had relied on. Then we seek what has always been there for us.

As I said, so many of the kids I grew up with became lost in one way or the other in their lives because they hated convention and ascribed to conventional ways of defeating it.

I remember a friend of mine, someone I took First Communion with in grade one, who, at seventeen, made a drug run, taking a pistol with him to shoot the man he was doing the deal with, if it came to that. Years later I met him hiding in his house, addicted to crack cocaine, the place filled with garbage and vermin. I think the drug trade offered this to all of us. It was once again the idea of the shortcut to nirvana. And he did nothing more than follow convention.

The con is always the same. It never tells us it is a con, and yet displays itself as one almost from the first. And it captured me in the same way.

Yet every once in awhile, in terrible pain, after drinking for days, I would see a child—or an innocent man or woman—and I would realize the terrible self-inflicted con I was perpetrating. That how I was living had nothing to do with what I sought—spiritual fulfillment—and that only a con more devious than any I had ever succumbed to before could make me think I was achieving something that, in fact, I was losing. And it led to the very sin I spoke about, and the very greatest of sins—the one that all sins aspire to. It is a kind of fulfillment that opposes fulfillment.

It was very strange, for at those moments, trying to write a book and clinging to the idea that I was seeking intellectual freedom, I kept a shotgun loaded in my study.

I was in deep despair in the winter of 1982. I did not see how I would live through another year.

Then one night I heard my mother's voice calling to me, as clearly as I heard my oldest son's voice downstairs a few minutes ago, though my mother had been dead five years. It was as if she was calling to me in alarm because I was no longer who I was supposed to be. I sat bolt upright in bed after hearing her voice, not because I had heard it—I knew I had heard it—but because of a much more important reason, I knew why she called to me.

The very next day a boyhood friend visited me with the

hope of letting me know I was drinking myself to death and would not finish another book if I continued. He explained to me as best as he could that I had that choice. The choice was very difficult because I was drinking so I would not have to write what I knew I must. And if I did write what I knew I must, then most of the people whose friendships and opinions I valued would almost certainly turn away from me. That was the secret of my despair, and over the years this was to happen to me.

And then this happened also.

It was a dream I had just before I began to try to change my life into a life where I could at least live. I know I have had this dream more than once when I was at the last of my drinking—but I did not know how to unravel it, or if it needed to be unravelled. I mentioned it briefly above.

This is what I dreamed—the man and the cart and the children, stopped by the solider. The interpretation is my own.

The most humble of men is taking his horse-drawn wagon, with his children, to safety. He has to cross a blood-stained battlefield. The children have faith in him, and he has hope, desperate as it may be, that he won't get stopped by the patrol. A young lieutenant stops him, and can either turn him in or let him go to safety. He looks at the man and sees in his humility, and in the eyes of his tattered children, something of the deeper meaning of the human race. The lieutenant decides to be charitable and he lets him go. In that one instance, faith, hope, and charity play out as the only three things by which the universe is measured. All the rest either relies upon these three things or tries to defeat them.

This is the recurring dream I had in bits and pieces over

that tumultuous time in my life. So what did it mean? I suppose it means a great many things.

Can say something about the children travelling along in the cart? Children are often looked upon with a good deal of skeptical irony because they are so often used, as Alden Nowlan said, "as dupes in a grown-up world."

Still, we might have the hope of the father riding the cart, but we will not have the faith of the children, for faith starts where hope gives out. The father certainly has his cross to bear. And there doesn't *seem* to be one miracle at the cross.

But "seems" is the word.

In a way, the lieutenant who lets them go finds out the same thing. I think he's an ordinary man, overcome not because of any great duty to humanity, but with compassion for the children. The children themselves are in tatters, scared, and they look only to their father. They have faith in him, who is defenceless. How can the lieutenant kill the faith of children in a man he could crush? He could if he did not realize that something more important and great than the bloody field—the human earthy field—was at stake, which had nothing to do with his career or his victory.

But the father in the cart is ready to die for these children, and to be—well—put on the cross for them. I do not know of any father—well, perhaps one or two—who wouldn't. That is the secret of faith and hope and charity in this little travelling cart. It is the same faith of the little boy taking his donkey to Rome.

Still, there is something else.

It is the children. These tattered children were a symbol of my faith at that time. Perhaps they still are.

This is what the dream was about—faith, hope, and charity—and I was being told from someone deep inside myself that I was not free.

"I believe steam engines and electricity show as much love of humanity as chastity and vegetarianism," Chekhov writes, disgruntled about an elderly Leo Tolstoy. That is, Chekhov says everything man aspires to has in its foundation the seedling that man is being faithful to some greater good. Chekhov knew this as much as any man who ever lived. So did the Tolstoy of *War and Peace*. But there is something else. Let us look at the two things Chekhov uses to rebuff what he considers Tolstoy's superficial ascetics. Steam engines and electricity. It is the first that was an invention, the second a discovery of what already was. And the invention could not have existed without the discovery of what was always there.

So, in some way, I believe that both were really discoveries of what already was—and always will be—and we must have the faith to discover these things, to reveal the world to ourselves—because it is, as Chekhov said, "One with love of humanity." Now we can do this as Tolstoy ascribed to at the end of his life—to give mankind up—or we can keep fumbling and struggling with the inherent faith that the universe is ours to discover.

But I want to mention this for another reason, because of the scientists themselves.

I believe no one can discover without faith. Sometimes these discoveries are thought to be because of our own

great ingenuity. But still we need faith to discover anything, and so any scientist has faith as a necessary part of
his inestimable credentials. If a scientist did not have faith,
then even the discoveries that came by accident wouldn't
have happened. No tubes or burners would have arrived at
the discovery, for no faith would have allowed the chance.

So any scientist who mocks faith has missed the most
valuable precept of his creed. It is not only science but faith
that science can work, which will keep us creating and discovering. (And the idea that many inventions are great puz-
zles we have been given to solve is another bit of proof that
we are in the presence of Something.) When we do discover
or invent, we will be inspired with, or by, a love of humanity. But any man working a pole in an ice storm in order to
restore electricity and get heat to a house with women and
children inside knows this.

"Eureka!" Archimedes says, and that childlike exclama-
tion echoes for over two thousand years. For it is science, it
is faith, and it is free—from everything pertaining to what
holds man back.

Archimedes was murdered during the Roman invasion of
his Greek island, while he was drawing a mathematical equation in the sand. His last words to the soldier who killed him
were: "You are messing up my equation."

"Men of my stamp do not commit crimes!"

Yes, they do, in fact, that's exactly what they do. And the
truth is that most of us, at least at certain times in our lives,
want to become men of that stamp, in one way or another.
It is not that we would commit crimes—hell, no. But we
would want to become men of that stamp. And if by chance

we do not see this, we confuse the issue of degree and kind, and liberty and power. We do not all become Napoleon, to the degree Napoleon did, or Hitler or Stalin, but we all have a chance to say, in betrayal of others, that we are men of that stamp and our betrayal is not a crime. So it is not a difference in kind, but only in degree. We might not wear the pompous hat or cloak, or build the wolf lair.

That is, in our betrayal of others—and betrayal in Dante's world is the worst of all possible sins—betrayal being the main plank in every sin's platform—there is a sense, even if a small one, that we are men of that stamp.

To counter the words "men of my stamp," and a million like it, God shows us that, for all our notions of greatness, nothing is as important as the immeasurable moment or the smallest of incidents.

You see, we cannot betray—it is almost impossible to betray when we are doing something for others. And real kindness can only be given with some understanding of child-like faith—that is a secret, too.

The most important thing is that the disavowal of the importance or true nature of faith is in many respects like the disavowal of electricity or the mocking of man's flight. We could not see them, so they did not exist. They were too fantastic or otherworldly to contemplate, and those who contemplated them were rebuffed and derided, until it became evident that they were present in our life and appeared whole before our eyes. Then our eyes were opened and, like startled and excited children, we saw for the very first time.

That is why "eureka" is so important a word.

I mention in books like *The Lost Highway* and *Mercy Among the Children* how Peggy's little cousin Wayne who mentioned to his mother their relatives in the room before he died; or how Anila's picture was found the very hour her daughter visited; or how my children themselves are easily dismissed. I know all that, and this is not a polemic to make anyone believe.

Still, I trust that faith effortlessly disables all that is thrown against it.

I have discovered that with faith the world is absolute and true. The mysterious becomes clear.

The child who was born far away from us is ours—the sanctimony of disbelief is defeated in a breath of air.

Faith has guided me away not from sin or wrong—never that—or from failing with my children, or my wife and I failing with each other—never that either—but away from what I had once believed in, that liberty was bought with power, and toward a more astonishing recognition of the sacred in our midst.

I know from experience that Something we pray to is well worth it. Something has always kept His promise, no matter how strange it comes about.

Made the lame walk, and, yes, the blind see.

David Adams Richards has received numerous awards and prizes throughout his career, and is one of the few writers in the history of the Governor General's Award to win in the categories of both fiction (*Nights Below Station Street*) and non-fiction (*Lines on the Water*). *Mercy Among the Children* won the Giller Prize in 2000 and was short listed for the Governor General's Literary Award and the Trillium Award. *The Friends of Meager Fortune* (2006) won the Commonwealth Writers' Prize for Best Book (Canada and Caribbean). His most recent novel is *The Lost Highway*.